GARH CI

Also by Robert Nichols

Slow Newsreel of Man Riding Train *
 (poetry, 1962)

Address to the Smaller Animals †
 (poetry, with Lucia Vernarelli, 1976)

Red Shift: An Introduction to Nghsi-Altai †
 (novel, with Peter Schumann, 1977)

Arrival: Book I of Daily Lives in Nghsi-Altai
 (novel, 1977)

*City Lights Books
†Penny Each Press

ROBERT NICHOLS
GARH CITY

BOOK II OF
Daily Lives in Nghsi-Altai

A NEW DIRECTIONS BOOK

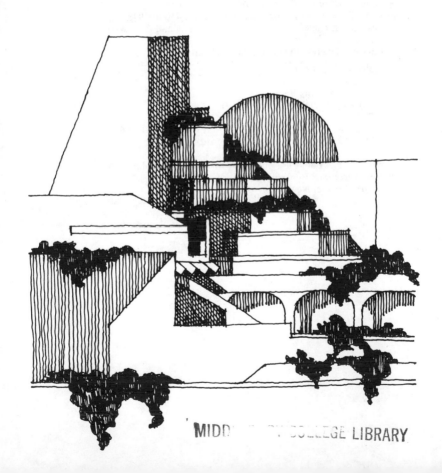

Garh City is the second book of the tetralogy DAILY LIVES IN NGHSI-ALTAI. I *Arrival*. II *Garh City*. III *Harditts in Sawna*. IV *Exile*. The first two books were published, respectively, in 1977 and 1978 by New Directions. The final volumes will appear in the near future.

Manufactured in the United States of America
First published as New Directions Paperbook 450 in 1978
Published simultaneously in Canada by McClelland & Stewart, Ltd.

Library of Congress Cataloging in Publication Data

Nichols, Robert, 1919-
    Garh City.
    (A New Directions Book)
    (Daily lives in Nghsi-Altai; book 2)
    I. Title
PZ4.N623Dai   Bk. 2 [PS3527.I3237]   813'.5'4s   77-13196
ISBN 0-8112-0654-8   [813'.5'4]

New Directions Books are published for James Laughlin
by New Directions Publishing Corporation,
333 Sixth Avenue, New York 10014

CONTENTS

To Mary Perot Nichols, Stanley Isaacs,
Stanley Tankel, and Jane Jacobs

IN THE DOLDRUMS

We have been here a year. The time hangs heavy. But there is no time. A wheel of seasons.

We have a new member of our Explorers' Party.

Jack Kerouac's death was extremely painful to us. But we have learned to do without him.

The people expressed their regrets. But soon after they seemed to abandon us to the chores of housekeeping in our baithak. Which is none too comfortable.

Alvarez is the active one. He manages a kind of official contact with the ganbus and is sent off on agricultural duties with one of the work sections.

One day we ran—quite by accident—into our third companion, William Morris. A rucksack on his back he stood in the Makers' Square with a guidebook. He had been examining the solar furnace in the blacksmith's shop and was much taken with it.

Regrettably Morris (another associate of The People's Voice), who had been scheduled to be sent with the original team, was blackballed by Alvarez. On the flimsy ground that Morris was a utopian and his naive brand of Christian socialism might prove a political liability.

We have abandoned our criticism/self-criticism sessions.

Meanwhile we have slipped into the habit of using the word "we" in the journal that is kept jointly. Is it that we are any less individuals? Perhaps not. On the other hand there is a common wave band, a range of vibrations, through which "Western eyes" *see* Nghsi-Altai.

So it is the local inhabitants who have defined the explorers.

• •

We have learned only one of the languages of Altai. But there are so many.

Sometimes the children come to visit us. It is easy to attract them with candy. On the other hand they prefer their own sweets—millet grains roasted in brown sugar. However, they are permitted this only on holidays.

Our expedition has been based here on the plains. That is limiting. We have been excluded from the other biomes—for what reason it is unclear. Long ago we applied for passports, but these were denied. Only Blake has made a short trip to the Drune forest. The Drybeds we have not seen, though this area is reputed to be the most advanced. Alvarez in particular is anxious to inspect the anarcho-syndicalist unions there.

It is mostly Morris who enjoys playing with the children. A knack. There was a time when the matriarchs tutored us (in Jat), encouraging us to open up, then laughing at our mistakes. Now we no longer make mistakes. Or they have other things to do than listen to us—notably refining and storing sugar.

Alvarez gives out proudly that he has been assigned to a county works project, after "meritorious service" cutting cane. Yet he is not as close to the ganbus as he would like. And he is beginning to sour on them. They are not as progressive as he first thought.

Blake has improved his playing the gusle. Joking, he says "it goes with the beard." But he has been drinking.

The meteorology station predicts that the rains are coming.

• •

Assauj (Sept.-Oct.)

A dreary day. Monsoon season is full upon us. The world is soaked. At four o'clock every afternoon the skies open as in a sluice, roads and landmarks are obliterated, the village becomes a sea of mud. Rain drums on the roof tiles. But our baithak is tight, though dark. No light through the straw shutters, and we sit huddled on the bamboo floor smarting from the flies that swarm up from below, from the cattle stalls.

Where has the time gone? We have spent several years here; can we say we have come any closer to an understanding of these people? They remain opaque to us, as is the landscape fogged by rain. They *resist* comprehension.

The original goal of our expedition: Discovering Nghsi-Altai. What a mockery the words seem. The deeper one goes into it, the more mysterious it becomes.

For a time we have seen little of Blake. He has been away visiting the sensor at the Soils and Weather Station. He returns at night, sometimes followed by Tattattatha's black leopard, which curls up on the bunk.

But today Blake is with us: the monsoon has confined him. He seems extremely lethargic...too much pulque...or can he have gotten a touch of malaria?

• •

Blake has been practicing solemnly on his gusle. He strikes the strings mournfully as if to resonate them against the rain, and he asks us if we'd like to hear a composition.

"By all means, sing it," Morris encourages him. "What is it called?"

"It's called 'The World of Nowhere.'"

Blake sings:

"No matter where you start
This world remains a place apart
Nothing to find here after your own heart.

"Everywhere your foreign eye,
Your foreign ear, no matter how they try
Catch no familiar gestures in reply.

"The people here pursue,
Even if its miracles you do,
A close serenity that puzzles you.

"As for the countryside,
So many trees brush your glance aside
Your greedy heart must go unsatisfied.

"Only, perhaps, across an opening lake
Some traveled echo of the search you make
Will send you homeward for perfection's sake.

"Be sure, this world of nowhere will expel
All who seek here a chance outlandish spell
That any place could offer just as well."

"A sad song, but appropriate. When did you compose it?"

"It's by a colleague of mine on Parnassus. Allan Hodges, English, twentieth-century."

"I don't like it all; it's too negative," Alvarez comments. Lacing up his boots, he stalks out.

"Of course the rhyme is a drawback. After the seventeenth-century nothing was quite right," Blake confided. "Would you like to hear another? This one is not mine either. It's called 'Europe,' by a Polish contemporary. Alas, I have forgotten his name."

Strumming the gusle, Blake sings a second song.

O EUROPE

O Europe is so many borders,
on every border, murderers.
Don't let me weep for the girl
who'll give birth two years from now.

Don't let me be sad because
I was born a European.
I, a brother of wild bears,
wasting away without my freedom.

I write poems to amuse you.
The sea has risen to the cliffs,
and a table, fully laid,
floats on foam among the clouds.

"So there you are," Morris agrees. "We are *between* worlds, the old and the new. And the borders of the one are as closed to us as the other."

The tonic of rhyme seems to have revived Blake. He adds lightheartedly, "But though the past is gone, we are still writing poems, and offer you still: A table fully laid/floating among the clouds..."

Alvarez returns with good news. He has been to the pan-chayat headquarters and has come to tell us our passports for the "closed biome" have finally come through. Our itinerary has been approved, and we are to leave for Garh City in three days.

So perhaps this signals a break in the weather.

ENTRY INTO GARH CITY

At the invitation of the Planning Ministry we have come to visit Garh. After a short trip across the plains, we arrived last night at the transportation node. Descending by skip (electric cable car) into the Rift canyon, we were plunged at once into the excitement and fervor of the big city.

The glare. A barrage of noise. Buildings of unexpected structure and function crowding the narrow area between the cliffs, connected by raised passageways. Everything compact, enormously compressed, "miniaturized." Yet they say this is a city of three million. An expanse of water in a canal is illuminated under a neon sign, lights flash on and off, the metabolism of urban movement, traffic. As the skip glided over the submerged rooftops, a tower loomed on our right. Within the steel frame was a cylinder of shifting, multicolored light, like a giant cathode tube.

Our guide informed us it was a "synerg" or public art object. "It registers the energy state of the city at a given moment traffic flow, heat, number of telephone calls, air composition index, even demographic information. The data comes in from the stations, is absorbed cybernetically, and emitted as light signals."

There arc no streets, no automobiles in Garh. Pedestrian and bicycle paths, called "meanders," wind through this inexplicable city. Rapid transit is by canals, which form the right of way for three kinds of traffic: boat, rail, and the ubiquitous air taxis.

We were taken with our luggage in one of these and soon reached a small hostel which is run by Intourist. It is to be our headquarters during our stay here.

A SWIM WITH ANARCHO-SYNDICALISTS

This morning we visited an anarcho-syndicalist club in the Third Ward. It is housed in a large building which contains a meeting hall, libraries, and data bank, and also health and recreation facilities. Here we were introduced to a number of Karst foremen. Unlike the Jat ganbus, who are inclined to be stiff, these talked to us readily.

Alvarez had been delighted to learn that the motto of the syndicalist unions here is "BEYOND SOCIALISM."

We were invited to take a swim in the pool before lunch.

"Do you swim well?" one of them asked. Alvarez, the activist, assented. Morris looked at him skeptically.

"Don't worry. We'll take good care of him in the water."

We were taken to the lockers, where we gave our clothes to a club attendant and started for the pool. One of our hosts stopped us.

"Wait. You've given him your money."

"I don't see how I'm going to take it with me," Blake growled. "Unless I'm to stick it up my arse."

"No, you'll be issued a pouch." We returned to the screened counter.

"Never trust a Karst. We Karsts make it a point of honor never to trust each other," we were told with a wink. In this way we were ushered naked toward the pool, with nothing on but our money belts like the rest of them.

The atrium of this workingmens' club is an airy space, under a high plexiglass dome. Forest trees in enormous pots cool and freshen the air. We were told the balconies cantilevered out from the sides contained restaurants and small sports arenas.

The pool was situated at the center of the space. On one side was the gymnasium. Here sweating Karsts were lifting weights, wrestling, and boxing. A group in toweled bathrobes sat in wicker chairs ranged in front of what appeared to be a teletype screen. "They are following the frontón game upstairs. Those are betting figures."

We were told that the insignia on the bathrobes indicated these were "Construction and Wrecking" workers.

Against the walls of the baths of veined and striated marble, the skin of the bathers glistened. There were only a few Deodars and Jats, the hue of their skins a cold blue and a warm chocolate respectively. The Karsts were a glaring white and somewhat translucent. All Karsts are albinos and have an unpigmented skin and startlingly pink eyes. They are of medium stature and have a curious barrel-like physique without extremities. No ankles or neck. The head seems to protrude directly from the torso. Their hands, which have a yellow palm stain and are webbed, stick directly out of their forearms like paddles.

In contrast our own band must have presented a bizarre spectacle. We were all painfully self-conscious. Alvarez like a small pugilist was the pinkest, with flaming ears. William Morris stooped and tried to be self-effacing—like all uncommonly tall men. He has ruddy skin and fine, rather pampered hands. Blake, with a long lumpy cock, is absolutely cadaverous. He stood with all of his ribs showing. We were all heavily mustached and bearded, whereas the Karsts and Jats are hairless.

However, none of the syndicalists paid us the slightest attention.

The pool seethed with swimmers. A game of water polo was in progress, pursued with utmost ferocity.

As Blake hawked up a cough which he disposed of in the scum gutter, Alvarez began dancing up and down on his toes and jabbing as if he were shadowboxing.

"Well, brother, are you ready to take the plunge?" one of the foremen asked him. And before he was able to answer gave Alvarez a violent push into the pool.

The Cuban was engulfed in the melée.

After a second he surfaced. His head popped out but was immediately grappled by a woman player. Caught in a headlock between her knees, he was submerged again. The scrimmage passed over them both.

Blake cried: "Good lord, save him somebody. He'll drown."

"Oh that comrade will take care of himself. He's spunky."

"They're only roughing him up a little."

The two surfaced. The wave of polo players moved on again. The filmmaker was pulled from the pool and lay on the tiles panting.

Our hosts gathered around him highly pleased. They kept congratulating him, shouting down at him: "SPRECCIA! SPRECCIA!" This is the highest compliment in the city. It means "spontaneous."

HOW WASTE IS HANDLED

There are no words in the Nghsi-Altaian languages for "waste," "rubbish"—everything is included under various aspects of recycling. Thus the system of waste disposal is called "urban mining," or alternatively "urban farming." In large measure this furnishes the basic materials for industry. Even the layout of the city into wards or geographical districts is determined by it.

We were taken to one of these wards to see the system in operation. First we visited the superblocks—clusters of dormitories and work places. Within each of these a number of contractors handle the disposal business: that is, collect rubbish from door to door (paying a good price for it) and also heavier jobs, then conveying it to the reprocessing depots. Work here is divided into four operations:

Cannibal Shop. For worn-out appliances and machines (refrigerators, communal T.V.'s, solar cooking units, etc.). These are repaired for block consumption, or salvageable parts are removed (cannibalized) and returned to the appropriate manufacturer.

Scrap Heap. In this section bulk materials are handled, with equipment for magnetic sorting, shredding and grinding, bailing, etc. Material is compressed hydraulically into standard shapes, then encased in concrete, steel, asphalt, or plastic. These are sold to the building industry. Broken glass and crockery are also reprocessed here.

Juicing Room. Paper and textiles are treated chemically and reprocessed.

Composite Materials Lab. Here new structural materials are made from old. Various materials form the "matrix": polyethelene, glass, nickel-chromium, ceramics, lead. To these are added the "compositing elements": in the form of fibers, particles, laminae, flakes, fillers, etc. Machine parts, plywoods, honeycomb structures are produced here.

In one lab, an engineering artel was making a multi-dimensional "organic" composite (Thornel 50) of graphite fibers embedded in epoxy resins. This is a high-strength metal substitute used for gas pipe. Yet the process is simple: the graphite fibers are produced by carbonization of rayon filaments. To be precise, by burning discarded stockings.

Blake conversed with a group of workmen in the Juicing Room, engaged in producing paper. The rag paper struck him as of good quality. He was pleased that they knew something of the process of engraving.

We stood at the door of the Composite Materials Lab at the end of our tour. Alvarez struck up a conversation with some of these "urban miners." He complimented them on the orderliness and what he called the "rationality" of the system.

"Yes. And there seems to be considerably less waste," Morris added. "Where are all the cans and cardboard boxes?"

Alvarez hazarded the explanation that in a nonmarket, regional economy there would be less need for advertising and transportation, and that this would reduce packaging.

The workers did not respond, apparently not understanding "packaging."

The following day we were given another demonstration: in the treatment of liquid wastes. There are two recycling systems. In the first are grouped processes having to do with cleaning and oxygenating the canals. The second, the "closed" system, deals with sewerage disposal and is referred to simply as "urban farming." The following are the steps in this chain:

Every ward has its truck farms. The vegetable produce supplies the neighborhoods and is also sold commercially on the free market. In Jat neighborhoods there are also roof farms.

These products are consumed; the waste (fecal matter, urine) is pumped·back to the farm area into settling lagoons. Here it is treated by bacterial action. Many types of bacteria are "raised" and in fact cultivated for specific functions.

From the lagoons the inert sludge is settled out, bagged, and used in soil conditioning. The effluent, rich in soil nutrients, is returned to the farms by a process of spray irrigation. The cycle repeats itself.

WE MEET UP WITH AN ARTEL

We are in a town square. Bands are playing. A speakers' platform from which oratory reverberates over the loud-speakers. An answering roar, armwaving and dancing by the population. Around peoples' shoes pigeons are scavenging crumbs.

In the Rift, politics seems to be a national game.

We are wedged up against the speakers' platform, the populace at our backs identified with the flags of the localities. The Syndicates and Communal Commandos are represented. They are wearing armbands of different kinds. A cheer bursts from the throats of a band of teen-agers.

As the rally breaks up we merge with the crowd as it streams out by the streets leading from the square.

After a quarter of an hour we cross a bridge. We are with one group, so it appears. The surge of people at our backs carries all of us along.

"Well, what was that all about?" Blake asked an older man.

We learn that it is a "seasonal demonstration."

If there is a further question it is unanswered. A vaporetto passes under the bridge at that moment and the steam, amplified under the trestle, makes a deep puffing sound. Then the canal boat emerges, its waves gently rocking the embankment.

The paraders are passing through a different ward, consisting of lofty superblocks. The street rises to a higher level. On both sides are the stores of Karsts.

The festival crowd has thinned considerably. The streets of this section are not full. There are no longer cafés or luxury shops, only local shoppers. The seasonal demonstration is far behind us.

Our own group to which we have attached ourselves are Karsts. All are dressed alike, including the women: buff or green short-sleeved jackets, shorts, and wooden sabots. There seems to be no differentiation among them except size. They walk at the same pace. But as we go on, several engage us in conversation. Blake, however, is uncommunicative.

Our straggling band of marchers turns into a lane between concrete walls as the street lights come on. The group keeps on silently with an air of letdown.

The narrow lane of the meander passes a series of juicing depots. We walk along in the line, no one seeming to notice us, or at least paying any particular attention.

However, as the meander comes out on a brightly lighted square with shops, the animation returns—they shout slogans led by the older cadre.

Our leader is a large man by the name of Bang. We learn that they were all from the same "Big Family/Little Family" group and are heading home to their own superblock.

Finally we arrive at another square. We stop before the burghall. It has begun to rain. We are invited in to dry ourselves and to have some warm ale.

A SPEECH TO THE COMMONS

Alvarez has gone several times to the burghall, which turns out to be called Red Cats. The place is both a restaurant and a meeting hall for the neighborhood Commons.

After our meeting with the artel in the square, we were anxious to become better acquainted with them. We went to the Red Cats one evening at Alvarez' urging.

The restaurant was open to the street, and there were café tables on the sidewalk under an awning. Beyond on a cobbled square a small band was playing, and acrobats were performing in a desultory manner for coins.

We entered to the usual amount of noise, which we have got used to in Garh. Orders for food were being shouted over peoples' heads. There was the clatter of dominoes and the added din of wooden shoes over the sawdust floor. They do not take them off in this public area. But what area here is not public?

"Big Bang," as he is called, was surrounded by cronies. The table was covered with beer mugs and plates of blood sausage. Our friend, who had been rattling a dice-box, stood up to greet us, extending his paddlelike arms.

"Welcome, citizens. Join us."

He and Alvarez gave each other the fraternal embrace, which consists of first shaking hands, then kissing each other on both cheeks and patting each other on the back, then shaking hands again.

"Yes, sit down. Draw up chairs. We're now in closed session here at Red Cats, but soon you'll have the treat of seeing an open session of the Commons."

We sat with them for the space of a half hour.

We were mystified as to who precisely the "Commons" were.

The room was filled with confabulating men and women, and even children. The superblock to which our artel friends belonged was having an informal meeting in preparation for the Assembly which was to be held the following week.

Big Bang was evidently a person of some importance—in a room filled with others of importance. People kept coming up to

Bang and addressing him as "citizen," bending down and whispering in his ear, embracing him in an effusive salute. Or someone would approach in a more deferential manner and say, So-and-so sends respects.

For a Karst, the leader was particularly slablike. A bald head, which he seldom moved, rested on rolls of fat welling up from his shirt front. He seldom used his arms either, preferring to make a point by heaving up his chest. His eyes were kindly and his skin mottled. He looked like some old seal.

Throughout the room, other clusters of tables also had their chiefs, a number of them women. Women like the men chewed tobacco, particularly when arguing. Spittoons were placed between the tables, so that during debates these areas were in a cross fire. There was a barrage of flying tobacco juice.

Bang circulated among the tables.

We heard the word "factions" repeated a number of times.

More trays of blood sausage were ordered.

A waiter squeezed by among the tables holding up a blackboard on which a list of items was written in chalk. At first we took it to be the menu. But it was a list of political items on the agenda for the Assembly.

The chief interest of our table appeared to be an addition to the municipal waterworks which was to come up.

Occasionally amid the rattling of dice and the clattering of dominoes, tempers flared on this question of the waterworks—or possibly it was some other issue. A small Karst ferociously playing darts in the corner made an impassioned challenge to the faction at our own table. We learned that this was "Short Wang," an inveterate opponent of Big Bang's.

During his attack, Wang choked with indignation, spat, and clumped with his shoes on the floor.

This orator·received applause. Several of the other tables even threw potatoes into the air. But there were some boos. Apparently the majority of the room was with our own faction.

The debate continued. Bang, leaning over to Alvarez, whispered: "I think we have them."

There appeared to be a general pleasure at our table for all the orators—even when they were opposing the Bang faction.

The orators marshaled sensible arguments—at least judging from the faces of the hearers. However, some local characters when they stood up met with catcalls and guffaws, no matter what they said. Evidently, they were known—and not to be taken seriously on any point.

Curiously, these were the people who spoke most vehemently.

This part of the program appeared to be a kind of screening process. No votes were taken. Yet the citizens did not seem to be making any effort to achieve a consensus either.

The point of the closed session appeared to be to explore conflicting points of view and develop opposing speakers, the more opposed the better.

It was approaching ten. The brass and percussion band playing in the plaza subsided by slow degrees; first the trombones and tubas, then the cymbals and French horns, leaving only the drums to accompany the gyrations of the acrobats. Gradually these stopped as well. The sidewalk diners began to shift their attention to what was happening inside.

Tables were pushed together, clearing a space in the center of the hall. A crew of television men began setting up its equipment.

Bang and the citizen known as Short Wang took seats in the center, assuming a dignified manner, their position "on camera" being arranged by the T.V. men. Both wore carnations in their buttonholes, we were told, so that these Red Cats speakers could be distinguished on television. There was also some posing of the crowd itself. The folk were not to be left out of the picture. Everyone appeared excited, and somewhat self-conscious.

A communications system connected this burghall with the others in the locality, known as the Redhook section. There were about ten neighborhoods or superblocks represented by the diners in the restaurants. Together and connected by T.V., these made up what was known as the Commons—now in session.

A screen had been set up from floor to ceiling. This was at first blank, then showed the synerg winking over the city skyline, evidently a signal. Around the main screen was a border of smaller screens. Framed in these appeared the gatherings in the other burghalls. Faction chiefs also were seated among their supporters, prominent with their boutonieres. As neighbors appeared and as familiar figures were recognized by the Red Cats, these elicited amusement and ridicule.

Our own group appeared in one of the side frames. When the light was on over this, Red Cats was on camera; that is, occupied the center screen throughout the whole system. (The system is called a "multicom.")

What followed was a wide-ranging exploration, and cross-discussion, of the issues that were to be on the agenda for the forthcoming Assembly. Differences on the items were ventilated. But here again we noticed they were in no particular hurry to press on to conclusions. For our own burghall, Bang appeared to represent the majority point of view, and Wang the minority; but both speakers behaved with more dignity than before. During the course of the debate—after the major speaker had made a point with especial eloquence—there was prolonged applause throughout all the Commons. Bang was presented with an umbrella, which he accepted but did not open.

Naturally, the times when our own speakers were on proved most interesting to the Red Cats. There was a period open to the floor. Much to our enjoyment a number of children spoke, and also one of the street acrobats. In fact, any speaker was welcomed. We were not a little surprised, at one point, to see Alvarez on his feet telling of his own experience as a cameraman in Cuba "when popular communications technology was not so highly developed" and complimenting the assembly on "escaping from capitalist atomization and on their revolutionary leap forward."

A DIRECT ASSEMBLY: MORRIS' NOTES

Approach to the stadium. Crowds. A holiday atmosphere. The meatpie peddlers. Our friends have brought along a keg of beer.

The stadium of the Fourth Ward dominates this section of the city. A huge berm rises over the hustling and approaching crowds. Pennants wave over heads, balloons float in the clusters held by the hawkers. The earth berm is about a hundred meters high and covered with grass; an occasional blotch of heather. At the base are the escalator entrances. A press here. The throng crowds to get in. Cards are being punched: the folk hand their cards over to half a dozen or so uniformed young men, who I am told are members of the Dog Society.

To vote is obligatory for every citizen in this direct Assembly. If one doesn't attend, one pays a fine.

• •

Once on top of the berm we find outselves on a wide promenade where the crowd circulates in two directions, observing each other. The crowd has thinned out here somewhat. Excellent view over the rim. The city drops away in a jumble of roofs and construction derricks. At the skyline one can see the stadiums of the other wards.

Sandwichmen move among the crowd. I see an old face, bleary eyes without interest. Yet the sign proclaims the Calendar of Events with the principal speakers in attractive block lettering. One can also buy printed digests—they are called "guides," giving a tabulation of the preliminary voting on the agenda items by neighborhoods.

• •

Our friends from Red Cats have come prepared for a long stay. They have great quantities of food in wicker hampers and even a portable refrigerator, cookstove, wet weather gear in case it rains, sleeping bags. (Alvarez has already picked up our sleeping bags at Intourist.) When we ask them jokingly where they intend to pitch camp, they motion down below among the tiers of seats. In fact there are already tents pitched down below there.

17

• •

Below us on the inside lies the great bowl of the stadium. It is a quarter mile across at the top. Not oval as I had first thought but circular. It is divided into sections by ramps. The seat tiers descend sharply to a center forum. The space around this is grassed.

I would say the stadium seats upwards of eighty thousand.

The rows of seats do not rise uniformly from the center but are terraced. About every twentieth or thirtieth row there is a wider platform. Here at intervals there are structures whose domes shine like onionskins.

There are about a dozen of these within the stadium, which we learn later are "city halls." There is an open plaza around each; that is, the promenade widens here. Directly below the tiers of seats rise more sharply. Thus the terracing in the stadium is not uniform but contoured.

A feeling of the basic architecture here: is it derived perhaps from the rice terraces?

Groups of citizens in front of the domes are spreading out their sleeping bags. Elsewhere large sections of the bowl are empty.

• •

Bang's niece has brought us to see one of the information kiosks. A crowd is around it asking questions. The clerks are at a counter, like a railway station. The kiosk is octagonal in shape with screens on top which I at first took to be advertisements.

But the citizens' questions are of a technical nature. Kikan (the name of Bang's niece) explains the kiosk is a data bank. There is an index of subjects.. With the help of the clerk one punches out one's question on the computer, and the answer appears up above on one of the screens.

We stand around Kikan—an attractive woman if somewhat self-assertive. To demonstrate the machine, she says: "What do you want to know? Ask it anything you like."

Blake says facetiously: "Tell me where is Fancy bred/or in heart, or in head?"

"No, it only has to do with subjects related to those coming up before the Assembly," Kikan replies sternly. "That kind of

18

question isn't in the data retrieval system. You'll have to ask it something else.''

The kiosks are surrounded by disputatious Karsts, arguing among themselves and pressing buttons.

• •

Alvarez has attached himself to Short Wang, who is prepared to address the Assembly. Wang will go down to the arena to join the long line of Commons' representatives who wish to argue some point or other. But first he must put his name on the waiting list and be given a number—his place on the speaker's calendar.

Meanwhile he struts around carrying a wicker hamper with a chicken in it which he will sacrifice to the Spirit of the Ward when his turn comes.

• •

Sporadic activity down in the arena, which we see far below. Acrobatic troupes of various neighborhoods are on display. Later in the day will come the principal teams of acrobats, those of the boroughs.

There have already been several votes, on the first items on the agenda presumably. These have elicited little interest among our own commoners. When a vote is announced, there is a call over the loudspeaker, which booms hollowly over the promenades. Then people go down and take their seats.

The voting procedure is as follows: If you wish to vote yes on a question, you stand up, wearing a green hat. When opposed—red. A simple and sensible method of mass counting.

Voting tabulation is done by sections; however, the sections don't vote as a block but by individuals. Thus one says, "The Fifth was carried by one thousand hats.''

• •

What is happening down there on the field? Considerable hoopla. The forum is filled, while below on the packed grass waits the line of prospective speakers.

It seems each faction chief has brought along his claque, consisting of private musicians and acrobats. Whenever a speaker is introduced a formation of drum majorettes wheels below the rostrum. Confetti is thrown up.

Can the band be playing Sousa? Squalls of applause drift up to us over the loudspeaker, but we hardly bother to watch these extravaganzas.

At night the public dances occur, performed by choruses of masked officials. But I have slept through two of these dance series already (in my Intourist sleeping bag) sufficiently exhausted by the day's excitement!

Politics as a tribal rite?

• •

A vote has been announced. Only a few moments afterward the tally is shown on the T.V. screens above the information kiosks. People applaud, munching hot dogs, a rucksack slung over the shoulder. And for some reason I am reminded of Aristophanes' description in *The Frogs* of the Athenian citizens coming to the Assembly with their "bottle of wine and three herrings."

Alvarez is contemptuous of the Athenian analogy. He suggests: Barcelona.

• •

In fact, the main action is not happening down there on the field—but up here, among the promenaders who are meeting, discussing, greeting old friends, etc.

Big Bang, as the Red Cats faction chief, seems to be at the center of this. The umbrella is unfurled at a certain point, which calls attention to him as one of Redhook's pre-selected floor leaders. One of the claque suspends the umbrella over Bang, while another holds the telephone by which he communicates with other chiefs. Both phone and umbrella are badges of office here. The telephone is used only for political purposes, there being strict penalties for private use.

• •

I note in these animated gatherings of people a general air of release, of expansiveness—everybody having been cooped up perhaps in their superblock apartments. I do not remember having seen any sizable parks or plazas throughout this city—in fact no public monuments.

So that possibly this stadium functions as THE public city space.

• •

What is my purpose in being here? Why am I setting down these notes? My eye is for the surface; I have perhaps some talent for noting similarities, metaphors. But should an artist be interested in politics?

I think so. What politics stands in *need* of now is metaphor.

Images of the city? The scene vibrates between contradictions. *Can* there be such a thing as a direct Assembly in a city of upwards of four million people?

At the same time I feel delighted to be a part of all this. But am I a part?

• •

Observations on city size.

Garh made up of ten wards, each ward of three hundred and fifty thousand. A total of three and a half million. But it is hard to see much beyond this ward. It may be the stadium that gives this impression of a self-contained process. The whole city is concentrated here, as under a lens. This impression is false perhaps.

Below the ward level are the boroughs and the neighborhood Commons. The smallest unit the neighborhood: about six to eight thousand people; meets at the burghall.

Singly, the neighborhood political organization is "a commons." When several meet together as during the open T.V. session—they become "the Commons." We are from the Red Hook Commons, or borough. Perhaps the section of the stadium we are sitting in is the Red Hook section.

In fact this is the case. We are told we are sitting in the Red Hook section and are shown its insignia. In this stadium ten boroughs are represented, each of approximately fifty thousand people. Ten boroughs together make up a ward. It is the Assembly of the ward which meets in this stadium.

It is clear to us that the neighborhood authority meets in the burghall. But is there some political unit or intermediate governmental body corresponding to the borough? I have not heard of any. If this is so, why aren't the neighborhoods and their chiefs—small fish like Bang and Wang—submerged in the ocean of the Assembly?

With all this—in order to govern a city of three and a half million—there does not seem to be any system of popular representatives. Everything is by direct vote, and I must confess this is incomprehensible to me.

• •

Third day. Alvarez sticks close to Wang, the orator. I am more interested in Big Bang, who is cast in the role of clubhouse organizer or boss. Bang is at the center of everything, but says little. Most often he is at his seat in our section of the bleachers, on the telephone.

At all times he is surrounded by a crowd of vocal Red Cats—a permanent distraction. In the middle of a phone conversation he will look down at the floor and scrape his shoe, as if trying to collect his thoughts.

Suddenly he gets up and announces he is going to speak with another community chief personally. Or is he going to "city hall?" He starts out and makes his way slowly around the promenade. But in the space of a hundred steps he is interrupted a dozen times. Finally he gives up and returns to his seat.

The ceremonies which take place down in the arena dominate the action at times. They appear to bore Bang. He plays dominoes.

Blake is fascinated by the stage happenings. These are on the wooden stage or forum, called for some reason the "congress." He enjoys particularly the choric dance rehearsals, which he goes down to attend. He has come back this time with a ceremonial mask. Also an article of dress which he claims is "a senator's." But the senators operate mostly at night, so it seems. At the same time Blake complains of the crowds. "They are stiffling him."

• •

Oratory is highly prized in the Drybeds. People keep coming up to Short Wang and encouraging him. "Give 'em hell, Wang."

His time to speak has finally come. As he prepares himself, throwing his cloak around him, the chicken's head sticks out between the ribs of the hamper with fierce unblinking eyes. Then we watch the three of them go down—Wang, Alvarez, and the rooster—descending from tier to tier of the immense stadium—

through the binoculars we have purchased at one of the kiosks.

But soon we lose them.

I am surprised to learn that Wang will speak in favor of the waterworks (which he previously opposed). The reason for this being, we are told: "discipline of the Commons."

•   •

Some metaphors:

1. Contours of the stadium—the rice terraces
2. Political activities here—the Athenian Assembly (doesn't 2 contradict 1?)

A possible analogy between engineering system (one of recycling) and the political system: This stadium is like a wheel with its numerous groupings, sections, etc. I.e., power is not a structure, but a set of relations between groups which rotates. In fact we are told that the senators "are the senators of the Rotary Club."

Power rotates. With each issue, a different set of officials?

•   •

Another vote has been called. This is announced over the loudspeaker, where we happen to be on the promenade gathered around Bang. Our cluster immediately breaks, and people rush to their seating section.

•   •

The politics of water. In this semiarid metropolis there are certain interests to be balanced. In Garh energy demand (which is local) conflicts with transportation, a citywide requirement. Must this be resolved by the faction chiefs?

Because of the canals being tied in with the energy-generating system, there are so many uses of water—for cooling, electricity, reservoirs, etc. The element water itself seems to be altered—because it is something the citizens determine specifically as to use. I suppose if I were a citizen of Garh I would actually *see* "a glass of water" in a different way.

•   •

Faces: In the Plains I was struck by the faces of some matriarchs. Here too in Garh certain citizens have a great air of authority about them—not only the cadre but ordinary commoners. Where does it come from I wonder?

The expression on these faces as if to say: "Nothing is delegated."

On the other hand are not these people—standing and palavering, and who are continually donning and taking off their green and red caps and munching sandwiches—somewhat ridiculous?

• •

I have now had a closer look at the city halls, those globe-like structures where the terraces widen. Each is about twenty meters high. My first guess had been that these were inflatable structures, the dome being covered by a light membrane. But no, they are permanent features of the stadium, and each contains a fully equipped amphitheater.

However, these are only in use during the day. At night the membrane retracts below the stadium surface.

• •

There appear to be television personalities in Garh. They are not stars of the entertainment world. Bang is in contact with one right now. Her name is Mrs. Zowie of the Flatbush borough. The face seen below an umbrella is sober. A wide, straight mouth gives the impression of frankness. Penetrating pink eyes, the white hair constrained under the peaked fatigue cap which is the ubiquitous insignia of the faction chief here. Suddenly after making a point Mrs. Zowie grins at us over the portable T.V. screen that Alvarez and I have clamped onto our seat. She comes in clear and inspires confidence—though I am told that Flatbush is pushing a proposal counter to ours.

• •

The fourth day.

We are told that the waterworks measure is coming up for a vote today. Bang is in an emotional state. He has spent half the night at the Redhook city hall whipping his borough supporters into line. From his seat command post he is in feverish communication with a score or so of his "fatigue caps" (community floor chiefs) in other parts of the stadium.

During each call he is surrounded by the local Red Cats gang, who keep giving him pointers. There is no letup. He appears exhausted.

• •

Apparently in the tangle of issues before the direct Assembly our own proposal is in difficulty. Our plan is for using the new canal to generate electricity (Bang and some of the Syndicate leaders want this for a processing plant). But this has run smack into another proposal: that of using the additional water for municipal swimming pools. Industrial growth is opposed to recreation. The health of the children is a charged issue. Mrs. Zowie has emerged as the children's champion.

●　●

I have followed Bang into the Red Hook city hall. In the dark I make my way toward the back. The small amphitheater rises sharply on three sides. The stage is filled with shirt-sleeved men and women. I recognize some chiefs from the television debate and others who have conferred in the bleachers with Bang.

Cigar smoke hangs in the air. On stage are the inevitable spittoons.

Excellent acoustics, voices carry easily from the platform, one doesn't have to strain to listen inside this structure. Hence its popular name—the "sneak chamber." The amphitheater seats about eight hundred.

Our chieftains are deep in formulating strategy—apparently to counter crippling amendments that have been added to the waterworks proposal. Bang, having disposed of a number of points, has now left the stage and taken a seat in the front row with some cronies.

A cry is raised: "Point of information. Point of information"—and a formal motion is made and passed for a film showing. This film is projected onto the stage so that it may be seen and debated in a manner similar to that of the Red Cats screening. Here the emphasis is less on personal style, and more technical. In fact every projection and statistic bearing on the waterworks alternatives may be laid out graphically. And with cybernetic controls, repeated at will. This is the same material available to the public at the kiosks. By now it has become boring.

Bang with his walrus hulk is on stage again, along with other figures from the Commons television debate. I am beginning to recognize a number of them. All wear their regalia.

Each faction chief has pulled into the amphitheater several of his personal claque, though the musicians are without instruments. Colorful as they are, these floor managers will disappear into the crowd when other issues are up for debate, their rank abolished as they set aside their umbrellas.

I realize with a shock that there are *no* elected officials in Garh. At least not in this ward.

•   •

The design of the structure of the city hall is interesting. On three sides the seats rise toward the back. At this point the supporting beams curve back in a sharp parabola and return to form the roof, where the trusses come together at the center. Here, in a kind of architectural feature or "boss," is suspended the communications control booth. The setup is similar to the multicom of the burghalls. The control projects the information and also brings onto the center screen, or onto those along the side frames, scenes of what is occurring in other parts of the stadium.

•   •

The Red Hook chiefs on the stage are conferring with those of another borough on the multicom. Their counterparts are down in another amphitheater, one of the city halls across the stadium.

Evidently we are in for a surprise. The word is we are to receive a visit of state. Mrs. Zowie is making a personal appearance, coming over from the Flatbush speak chamber on the other side of the stadium. I am told that such visits are unusual, though not extraordinary.

Mrs. Zowie arrives and is welcomed onto the speaker's platform with applause—which seems strange, considering the Flatbush stand on the canals.

But Mrs. Zowie's speech is conciliatory. A deal has been made apparently. Both Bang's plant and the children are to be taken care of.

•   •

Now the vote is in. We watch the official counting on the center T.V. screen. The boroughs were fairly evenly divided. But with the help from Flatbush the amended Redhook proposal has carried by "three thousand hats."

• •

Night time. The balance has returned in Nghsi Altai after the pandemonium of the day. The eyes of eighty thousand spectators in the stadium are concentrated on the circle of the arena which glows below.

This forum at night becomes the Congress. The ceremonial dances are held here which express, in music and pantomime, in the amplified masks of the senators of the Rotary Club, the political votes which have been ratified. On this last night what is being performed is the "Fourth Dance House."

We stand thus in the bleachers, the hundred refractory struggles and acrobatics of the day muted, and the communities hushed. The burghalls are merged. The globes of city halls, sliding on their retractable frames, have sunk into the floor. They have simply disappeared from their various levels and locations on the promenades. The stadium is now one, a single concave shape that contains the whole. It is a great bowl of darkness with the pinpoint center of the dances.

The people in conclave. But is this all?

What do the dance houses mean? Blake is down there somewhere. Alvarez and I walk along the upper promenade. By the edge of the grassy berm we look out over this City of the Ten Wards—where the lights of the other stadiums glow over the rooftops. Are assemblies being held there also?

BLAKE MOVES TO A REST HOUSE

During Asauj, Blake moved out of Intourist. He has been living at a rest house sponsored by a sect of the Deodar priesthood. "It's quiet at least. What a relief to get away from all those guides," Blake tells us. Here is an account of the Ekwensi rest house:

The Ekwensi priesthood, a branch of the Wilderness Society, operates in all city wards. Because of the fast pace in Garh and the tendency of its citizens to hysteria, these missions are conceived of as providing relief from urban stress. Shelters are operated in each section, generally near the business center. A small fee is charged. The patrons are businessmen, operators from small plants who come during the work break, shoppers, and even neighborhood children.

Upstairs there are a few rooms for "foreign persons," who have a privileged status in Nghsi. Below, an attendant who presides over the rest room, which is called ku-man-senu: literally, "shadow-sound bath."

They operate in this way. One enters, takes off one's shoes, and is assisted into a full-length burlap sheathe which fits over the head like a potato sack. The senu is a raised stage about the size of a boxing ring enclosed on four sides by walls also of burlap. Once inside the enclosure one simply sits or lies on the mat. A changing light pattern is thrown onto the screened walls from outside. The pattern is abstract, though occasionally there may be projected a phrase or specific word MILK AMETHYST). Simultaneously there is a sound projection from speakers mounted at the corners, the circular loop repeating itself. The sounds are also abstract: mysterious, persistent—like a frog pond at night.

The effect is quieting, Blake says. One can see out of these burlap sheathes, though the vision is misted. But one cannot be seen. There are generally not more than six or eight persons admitted at the same time. One feels physically in contact with them, yet at the same time invisible. In Blake's words: "I have rested here often. Closeted within my hood, I had the feeling I have had so often in Nghsi-Altai, of being anonymous—of having *lost my own individuality* and being immersed in some deeper and mystical community."

Talking is forbidden. Then, when people come out of the ku-man-senu and take off their sheathes, they will smile at each other, touch each other on the shoulder, and go their own ways. Blake will go up to his own room and play the gusle or do some engraving on a plate.

But he is always being interrupted. Curiously enough there is no word in the Karst language for "privacy."

ALVAREZ' DESCRIPTION OF THE BANG COLLECTIVE

HIS FIRST LETTER: ON DORMITORIES

Dawn-Is-Red Superblock
Eighth Ward, Garh
Redhook Commune
5 Baisakh

The People's Voice
9 Rockefeller Plaza
New York, N. Y.

Saludos Compañeros:
　　Since I last wrote I have moved out of Intourist. I'm living in a workers' collective on the opposite side of town. During the last months I have seen little of Blake and Morris. Frankly, that's a relief.
　　I am now a full-fledged member of a working peoples' artel, live with them in one of their dormitories. See above address at which you can write me. And have even been assigned a wife.
　　Would anyone have imagined this a year ago? It's like shedding your own skin. No more foreign observer role for me. I have thrust myself forward full speed into the life here. I hope I have become that *new man in the making*. "In the making" is the operative word here. There is still some distance to go.
　　First, let me tell you how all this happened. I wrote about our meeting with Bang's group. We joined them one day on a parade, and followed them back to their neighborhood. Well, I soon became friends with the old man—I guess he's some kind of political boss, or ganbu. And politics is everything here: It's like baseball back home.
　　In any case it was not hard to become accepted. People here pride themselves on getting along with foreigners (we are made pets of). And Bang is naturally gregarious. It wasn't long before

I became a member of his band of cronies. When I arrived at the commons, there was always a place for me at the table and a mug of beer.

Well, I can see you fellows asking, what's it like to have a native wife? You can get that idea out of your head immediately: These people are very sophisticated. Typical city dwellers. As for the women's looks, they're not that bad either. On the streets they wear one thing, at home another. At home they like to dress up, put on make-up. The first thing a Karst woman does when she gets through the door is put on bright lipstick and cheek rouge.

With their white skin and hair sticking up out of their head like bristles, they look like dolls. They also like frilly things. I bought her a pair of nylon panties at the American gypsy quarter. She was wild about them.

Life in a dormitory. First of all we're all crammed together in what is called a "sixteens": That means sixteen "pairs." But also there are a good many children and older people. We share the same space: eating, sleeping, socializing—and also work. This is the meaning of an "artel." Am I correct in thinking that *this* is the fundamental unit of communism?

I have just learned another name for the dormitory: "Big family/Little family unit." The "Big family" refers to the room where the common activities are. This is two stories high. Around it on a second level are the cubicles occupied by the pairs. These are pretty damned small. In Kikan's and mine— only enough space for a bed and bureau. Luckily the children aren't here during the week; they're off at a "child center." When they do come on week ends they sleep on the floor of the balcony on mats outside the cubicles. I hear it's noisy: pillow fights, throwing spitballs across the balcony, etc. Not something I look forward to.

(resumed later 10 Baisakh)

This week end Kikan's children came for a visit. I had been apprehensive: You know how children are—my not being an albino and speaking with what must seem to them an outlandish accent. But they were delighted with my pink skin, pulled my mustache, and even called me "Father." As they do with all male members of our "sixteens." They make no distinction it seems.

I must sign off now—the bell for an exercise period.

(resumed 12 Baisakh)

I'd say the big experience here, living in the Dawn-Is-Red Superblock, is going up and down elevators. I may have mentioned, the city is on multiple levels—not just the apartment and business buildings, even the parks. One is always whizzing from one level to another on an express elevator.

Our apartment building is typical of those in the Eighth Ward (one of the older wards). It's about thirty stories high (but on the fifth "city level"). The building is a central spine or mast (with elevator and utility core inside), around which the dwelling units wind in a helix. The apartments are globular like pumpkins and hang from the structure from a single stem. They are called "pods."

Within ours, the divisions in the upper story dormitories are formed by the pumpkin ribs. Below is the common space. From the commons there is a companionway leading to the elevator. Another leads outside to the "terrace."

But these terraces are huge—they are more like hanging lawns. Each artel has one, suspended in air. So as one looks outside, this is a major feature of the cityscape. From our window one sees literally hundreds of these hanging outdoor terraces, almost always full of people.

I have already started my training sessions with the artel. But of this more later, in a following letter.

Till my next, fraternalmente,
Santiago

THE SECOND LETTER

Dawn-Is-Red Superblock
Eighth Ward, Garh
15th Jaith

The People's Voice
9 Rockefeller Plaza
New York, N. Y.

Saludos:
    I have decided to work hard eradicating individualism. This must be my number one priority here if I am to become a real member of the collective. I had thought with my socialist background I had come a long way. But I still have some antisocial habits apparently, so my "wife" tells me.
    For instance, Kikan has been complaining of my smoking in bed. And she's right. Our cubicle is not designed to accommodate my corona-corona cigar. It smokes up the whole balcony, and soon all the other "pairs" are coughing. But the other artel members' habit of chewing tobacco communally is repulsive to me.
    I have promised Kikan I will reform.
    You ask in your last letter what the Bang Artel does during the day? Here is the daily schedule (brief outline):
    Up at dawn to the sound of a sonar gong (which wakes the whole superblock).
    Immediate assembly on "the nets" (outside parks). The spectacle of the entire borough doing mass calesthenics.
    Following this we break up into small groups for self-criticism sessions. Delegates are elected to the public works organizing committee. Then we descend to our commons. At breakfast, sitting around the table, members of the artel tell each other their last night's dreams. These are commented on.

A work-study session is called after this. Economic exercises. We "simulate" class and production relations to be anticipated in that morning's business with the Syndicates. Group calisthenics.

Second and Third Age Groups go to a superblock Maintenance Center and to the Spray Farm. Exhortation by "veteran workers." Assignment of the afternoon tasks by delegates who have returned from the public works organizing committee of the superblock.

Then our artel goes off to its places of work, generally by vaporetto, carrying box lunches and with much talking and shoving. The artel goes as a body, men, women, and veteran workers, and some children who have been designated "observers."

In the afternoon the public work of the municipality is done. I am not clear as yet as to the distinction between "public " and "private."

I've been getting on fairly well with Kikan—though we have ideological arguments and disagree on certain points. She loves to argue (she is Bang's niece). But affably. I sometimes wonder whether these Karsts take their duties as a revolutionary vanguard seriously.

In the evenings—exhausted from training—I relax in the common room and play "go" or six-handed cribbage with my "children." I've become their favorite father. The name of my eldest son: Kao. A strapping boy—a hellion.

And I have a daughter called Peach Blossom. I am going to school with Peach Blossom.

And by the way, "school" here seems to mean "child labor"! Is this possible? After leaving our pod we go to the superblock Maintenance Center and simply perform chores.

This brings me to the subject of artel training here in the Drybeds. The subject is mystifying—if one can use this word in a socialist society which is supposed to be clear and rational. Perhaps it is rational for the Karsts.

They are a food-producing artel. What techniques, what training does this entail? On this they will not enlighten me, saying I "must learn the general things first" and "perform the exercises." The exercises are as follows: We all climb out the window onto the terrace and throw ourselves into it—men, women and children, grandfathers and grandmothers! All are very agile and coordinated. There are dances in the style of folk opera, "Cutting Maize," "Planting Rice Shoots," etc., accompanied by songs. Then, there are the "body economy" exercises. These are slow, similar to tai-chi. But what is the relation to food production?

As for the "general things" I suppose they are inculcated at the Maintenance Center school: labor discipline, working with others in common tasks (praxis). This alternates with classroom studies on an abstract level. Certain "earth sciences" are taught, biology, plant physiology, nutrition, the mathematics of growth, Newtonian physics, etc. The Karsts breathe in the sciences like air.

I was touched the other day to find out that my daughter, age eleven, is memorizing for her language studies stanzas from Calderón. The teacher has a wretched Portuguese accent. Fortunately I was able to help her, and she helped me with the Second Law of Thermodynamics. We are in the same class—both being Third Set Apprentices.

All the age sets in the artel are studying heat. The method of advancement is bizarre. In the Drybeds "ideas" are considered property, at least as a kind of group privilege to be taken over by one group from another—like medicine bundles among the American Indians. Thus, when I reach the Fours, my son Kao (who is now fourteen, a grade ahead) will confer on me the Third Law of Thermodynamics.

(continued 15 Bhadon)

I am advancing rapidly. Have already passed through Grades Three and Four. In fact the whole artel praises my enthusiasm. Bang predicts that I will soon be in the Fifth and a mature proletarian.

And then I shall go off to work with the artel, after breakfast.

I am told a curious thing about the Fives. They operate a "space and technology lab": that is, machines are studied not for their mechanical functions but as they affect work space and the emotions of the operator. How people can reach and stretch, pass things on to each other pleasantly, communicate instructions directly, etc.

So—rapidly I advance. But I am sorry to say that Kikan is less encouraging of my progress than some of the others. She warns that I should not be overcurious and push myself into mastering the applied sciences too fast, before I have learned "correct attitudes."

Does she resent my advancement? As for correct attitudes, I am sure I cannot be faulted on this score!

Fraternalmente, your compañero,

Santiago

THE ZIMBABWE STEEL MILLS

We have been taken to visit Zimbabwe, the great steelworks on the city's outskirts. But there are two "Zimbabwes."

The plant is in a section of the Rift called the Dolomites. How pleasant the trip there by canal, almost like one of those enchanted rides of childhood. The scenes changed as we passed through the various city sections, which revealed themselves to us afresh in shifting perspectives. Our vaporetto chugged placidly along the embankment, past rows of point houses, the images of trees and strollers reflected in the water below agitated by our own waves.

"Old" Zimbabwe used to be the principal steel mill in Nghsi-Altai in the days of the National Industrial System (before the economy was regionalized). Now there is a new, smaller, and more efficient mill nearby—a so-called "natural energy" plant. The old rolling mill, now become an antiquity, has been preserved as an industrial park and is used for cultural and recreational purposes.

Like a moon landscape this dolomitic area seems to the beholder a proper setting for steel-making. The bare walls of the canyon tower above, where birds scream. The surface is composed of beaks and volcanic craters, with every once in a while a geyser shooting up. The color of the earth is salt. Curious domes, fossil trees are the only architecture.

We passed through this and came to the old park. Here we glided along the shore for several miles, the steam from our funnel drifting over the ancient works now interlaced with trees. The old blast furnace was a skeleton, girders and roofs twisted and surrounded by slag heaps. A pitted slab. Some remnants of the original cranes and rolling presses. Occasionally we came upon a group of sightseers gathered around a cultural exhibit. The bulk of the site of the obsolete rolling mill, which used to be a mile long, has been converted into a soccer field.

"We don't have anything this big any more, and it's not the

custom these days to build with permanent materials. It's really a museum piece," our guide informed us during a brief lecture.

A hawser was thrown ashore. We were winched into the dock with much shouting.

• •

Here on the opposite bank of the canal is the new steelworks. We visited it next. This is a geothermal plant; that is, run by the earth's steam, which is tapped from a lower layer where the heated rock acts upon subterranean water. This "geotherm" lies everywhere under the Rift and is tapped through boreholes. These pressure points are capped, and the power is led through ducts to the plant.

As we came up from the landing, these ducts ran everywhere over our heads. The steam is led into the superheaters where it is "boosted" from a temperature of four hundred degrees centigrade at five atmospheres to the temperature and pressure required by the turbines. The turbines, which we were told were "single-reheat turbosets," power a generator developing a hundred megawatts of electricity.

"Now would you like to see the furnaces?" Blake said he was interested, so these were exhibited next. The small electric smelter, a standard item, is first charged with scrap, then molten iron, then carried along and subjected to a process called "the blow." Pure liquid hydrogen is injected and the impurities are oxydized. Then the poured steel is batched: carbon, manganese, and other elements added to produce the required alloys.

Another feature is the elimination of the long continuous hot-strip rolling mill and its replacement by a smaller planetary mill. In this the plate is pulled under pressure in opposite directions through a series of rotary gears, and thus rolled to size and tempered. This type of mill is in general use throughout the many regions of Altai.

A meeting with the management had been scheduled for us. However, we were first taken on a tour of the plant vegetable farm, which is operated in conjunction with the mill. Mostly cabbages are grown here in the mineral-rich irrigated soil running along the canal bank. The crop about to be harvested, and the green, placid rows surrounded the steel factory like an inland sea.

It is mostly Jat in-city immigrants who work on the farm. The plant also runs a professional sports league, staffed for some reason by Thays from the Drune. Together these three enterprises make up the Zimbabwe Association.

• •

We had been granted an interview with the two officials who head the Supreme Committee or Committee of Commitees that runs the steel plant. But they were at a meeting, so we waited. Finally the two men arrived together followed by a crowd of associates, stenographers, and what seemed like a press corps with video crew. All were talking at once. Liu Shao-shi, the manager, had a top hat and was dressed in a striped swallow-tailed coat. He was introduced to us and nodded in an exhausted manner, at the same time mopping his face with a red handkerchief. The second official, introduced as Lin Piao, wore a full field marshall's uniform.

"Be with you in a minute. We have to sign some decrees."

"We've just come from a conference with the Planning Committee."

The video crew completed its business. Liu posed at his desk with Lin Piao a respectful distance behind. The decrees, signed, were carried by cable T.V. throughout the branches of the Association, we were told, in a simultaneous translation into three languages. Finally everyone left except one of the secretaries. Liu Shao-shi stripped off his jacket with relief and grinned at us. Lin Piao had already taken off his, revealing underneath a rather dirty woolen undershirt. They broke out a bottle of whisky and the interview began.

"So you are the syndicalist group from the United States. You're interested in how we operate here? Go ahead. Shoot. Ask anything you want."

"We are not all syndicalists," Blake remarked. Morris complimented him on what they had seen of Zimbabwe. Alvarez asked about the Association, "Was it large?"

"About twenty thousand workers," was the reply.

"Your committee manages this enterprise; it is under yours and Mr. Lin Piao's direction. Yet you have these positions only temporarily, as I understand it?" Alvarez pursued.

"Yes. The leadership is rotated. Everyone has a crack at it for a time. I have another term to go. Then thank God I'll be rid of it."

"So, after that you'll be back at your regular trade in one of the departments. What is that?"

Liu was a welder. He rolled up his sleeve and showed us his heavily spotted upper forearm. He told us this was caused by the sparks from the welding torch getting inside his leather protection gear.

Lin Piao's trade was "metallurgical chemist." He also expressed a desire to get back to the shop and complained that "management was an awful headache."

Alvarez complimented them on their trades, then gave them both the fraternal salute he had learned at the swimming pool.

Morris said: "I'm intrigued at this rotation business. With us, we have trained people, managers, to run the day-to-day operations of our plants—which after all are pretty complex. You don't think that a specialist is required?"

The word "specialist" drew a blank. Lin Piao merely stared at us, while Liu scratched his behind.

"You're speaking of a class of people who do nothing but manage the whole time?"

Liu seemed nonplused by the idea. He acknowledged the advantages of brains. After all, one didn't make steel with a bunch of dumbbells. Every worker had to be trained, and promoted according to his skills—but that was the business, wasn't it, of the departments?

Lin Piao, who appeared the theoretician of the two, asked us whether it didn't seem to them "risky"—a permanent management. Work was work; but running things and "the management of one group of men by another—well, wasn't that a political question?" As such it was better handled by rotation.

"So it would be fair to say that you have a hierarchy of skills, but not of power?" This formulation seemed to please Alvarez.

Blake asked how the heads of the Committee were chosen. Liu said they were chosen by lot, or "by the bean."

"By the bean?" the engraver asked, his eyebrows raised.

The manager explained. There was a jar of beans. The Committee members were led up blindfolded. If they picked a colored bean, they were chosen.

This applied only to the Supreme, or Executive Commitee, called the "Prytaneia," which was rotated every six months among the principal groups of artels. In the other committees—chosen for a one year term—the officers were nominated and selected by a show of hands.

Together all of the committees made up what was called the "Boule" or "Syndicate" which ran the plant.

"What are the duties of the executive?"

The manager described them: seeing to it that production schedules were met, labor discipline, and the making of "short-ranged decisions—subject to ratification by the assembly."

Blake asked what was meant by labor discipline.

"Well, mostly imposing fines—for absenteeism, carelessness in handling equipment, etc. In some cases an employee is beaten ..."

"Beaten!" Morris interjected. "How barbarous."

Liu hastened to reassure them on this point. If he felt wronged, the worker could petition for redress of grievances of the next General Assembly of Workers—which met every ninety days. If the managers were upheld that was the end of it. If not, they were fined or themselves beaten.

Alvarez, approving this procedure, said it was harsh but fair. He went on to ask about the other committees.

Lin Piao ran through these. They were: the Planning Committee, in a way the most important, as of course "everything had to follow the production plan," the Committee on the Agenda, the Committee on Industrial Relations (meeting with the shop stewards in the departments), and the committees on Finance, Statistics, Sports, Farming, Research and Development, and on Municipal Affairs. There were a few others. However, Lin Piao insisted the duties of all these committees were not great. The steel plant "pretty much ran itself," and the members of the Boule were merely delegates. Ultimately they were responsible to the General Assembly of Workers, which met every three months in the sports stadium.

"The sports stadium—ah," Alvarez remarked. "And there every worker has a voice?" The manager nodded. Blake said, "It must be pure bedlam."

To Morris this seemed a rather unwieldy arrangement. He asked how it worked. Wasn't it difficult to make decisions?

Lin Piao acknowledged this. However, he insisted there were certain customary rules and procedures according to which the Assembly, or "Ecclesia," as it was called, functioned. He explained as follows:

The Assembly met, and the first order of business was a vote of confidence in the executive officers.

After that there were reports by the committees, the Finance and Sports committees being generally of the most interest.

Then there was new business—all proposals having been first submitted to the Committee on the Agenda and then posted for a week previously on the shop bulletin boards. Lin Piao explained that any workman could make a proposal and speak for it. This was called "right of initiative." The proposal carried the workman's name, and he had to be responsible for it. In other words it had to be positive--for a capricious or sectarian proposal an initiator could be fined or beaten.

There was also the "right of amendment"; that is, to offer a counter proposal and argue for it.

After these popular debates, the motion was referred to the Prytaneia, the chief officer of which (in this case Liu Shi-shao) would be presiding. But the Supreme Committee had no right of veto. It could either approve or offer the motion to the floor "without conclusion."

The Assembly thus decided each proposal by vote.

This account delighted Alvarez, though he had been apprehensive in the beginning. He clapped his hands and shouted: "Bravo! Bravo!"

Morris also was pleased. He said he would like to see a plant
Assembly in action.
Liu answered, "I can tell you, it's something!"

• •

After lunch at the Zimbabwe sports club (the welder and the
metallurgist had donned uniforms again) Blake said to Lin Piao,
"So you feel you have achieved workers' self-management? And
by God, everything is managed isn't it? One swims in the
canals; the ruins of blast furnaces are parks; even the city air is
clean."
Alvarez asked him if he missed "the dark satanic mills?"
Pensively the seer had been looking out the window at the
cabbages. "I do not think we have arrived yet at the New Jeru-
salem."

• •

Alvarez and Morris engaged each other in argument. It was
clear there had been Karst improvements in metallurgy, but
what about the ownership of the means of production? Morris
explained his views:
"For instance, I myself had a small textile plant, in which
we wove fabrics. We had, I like to think, an advanced attitude;
the workers were trained in a creative and craftsmanly approach; we encouraged participation, group discussion, etc. But
still: it was I who owned the plant and the looms. I don't think it
would have occurred to any of us that it could be otherwise."
Alvarez: "And you call yourself a socialist?"
Morris thought the question of ownership was probably ir-
relevant in the Drybeds. Property would be a resource, as among
the Jats. Even the property of a steelworks and the improvements made on it through capital investment would be like an
agricultural plot with its improved soils: it would be considered
to be held in common.
Blake asked: "Who owns Zimbabwe?" Still looking out the
window he replied with a poem extemporized:

"Who owns Zimbabwe?
The sky. The sky owns Zimbabwe
through its smoke.

Who owns Zimbabwe?
The lake. The lake underground owns Zimbabwe
through its steam.

Who owns Zimbabwe?
Who owns Zimbabwe?
The slag heaped on the earth owns Zimbabwe.

The fires inside the smelter own it.
But not the hands that set the fires.
Nobody owns it.
Nobody owns Zimbabwe."

Morris returned to his own defense. "Yes, I called myself a socialist, but there cannot be only one socialist enterprise." He went on to say that that solution was not feasable unless general. His mill had been after all located in England, and when a weaver left for one reason or another and went to work in some textile plant elsewhere, he was penalized. Being nourished in a co-operative attitude, the poor man was even more alienated from his machinery. He was even worse off than before.

Lin Piao, who had been listening, asked in surprise, "You mean an individual worker can hire himself out to a plant?"

The idea struck him as entirely novel. Liu explained that in Nghsi it was the artel as a whole that was employed. The idea of an "individual employee" was unthinkable.

"Unthinkable?" cried Morris. "Then who is it that is hired?"

Piao offered his own case. He said his own artel had first discussed "buying into" the steel plant and whether they had enough capital. Then they had made a proposal to the industry and had contracted to take over part of the operation in return for profit.

Alvarez asked, "So you bought into it. And for this you put up your own capital. But what is that?"

"But of course. The capital is our artel." He explained that they were members of the Fire and Metals Brotherhood—of which there were numerous branches. As such they possessed "certain aspects of scientific knowledge and certain skills ... In short, we had a good deal to offer."

"How does this work practically?" Morris protested. "After all, we're not dealing with a primitive operation. Here it is not a matter of a group of laborers having a few small tools— a scythe or a pickax, or even a tractor or payloader which they can bring to the job; but of a complicated technology. Let's say your artel arrives at this steel mill and contracts, as you put it, to operate the reduction furnace. How do they know how? And this is tied to other skilled operations: operating cranes, batching mixers, crucibles, etc. In short, a production line. Does the whole assembly shut down, while they are being taught to do this?"

Liu said he saw no problem. Of course there was a brief training period. But production went on. And he added that it "was quite customary for members of the old artel, who were of course of the same brotherhood, to train the new."

"But why would the old artel be replaced? And why would they want to go elsewhere?"

"One can't go on making steel for a whole lifetime."

Lin added, "That would be boring. It would lack spreccia."

Morris rose. "But we must be taking up your time."

Both the president and the chairman of the board smiled broadly. "The plant closes in the afternoon."

COUNTRY HARDITTS IN TOWN:
THE FOREIGN QUARTER

Each ward has its foreign quarter in Garh. In the Sixth Ward it was the Kansu-Hardan Quarter, named after a locality in the plains. Many of its inhabitants had come here. The Sandranapaul Harditts lived in Kansu, in the Grain of Millet Superblock overlooking one of the canals.

In the foreign quarter the buildings were of the Jat type. They were not the high cylindrical point houses with their tension masts but were of middle height and joined together in the country manner, with wide roofs for chicken or turkey runs and vegetable gardens tended by the commune.

One room in the apartment was the Shrine Room. Though for the worship of the Ancestors, it was set aside for living guests—meaning Sawna relatives during the great city festivals. During much of the time the room was empty and had a sacrosanct air. On the shrine joss sticks burned in polished brass jars before photographs of the Ancestors. The family crowded into the remaining three rooms. The grandmothers, also Sandranapaul and his wife Olga, slept on planks which were put against the wall each day. The rest slept on the floor on bedrolls.

Sometimes the younger members would complain of these arrangements and point to the prevailing city customs, which they felt superior. Then either Olga or one of the matriarchs would say: "I don't care how the Karsts live. Let them be as practical as they like. We have our own obligations."

Venu and his family arrived for the Fourth of July-Ten. It was here, at Grain of Millet, that Venu had boarded during his factory year at the age of fifteen. And had been given his first sexual experience, sharing with this same Tatti Olga his initiation halvah. This was the custom in Kansu. But it was also customary to keep the seduction secret. Thus to Venu the memory of the halvah had a peculiar sweetness.

However, he found his tatti had grown fat and was much given to moralizing—like her mother.

There were a dozen or so Sawna relatives. Venu and Sathan brought their three children. There was Sathan's older sister, Nanda, with her children, but with no husband. The elderly Bai had been left behind because of her phlebitis. The matriarch's sister, Helvetia, was very much present, growling in a deep voice and shouting out instructions from the moment they arrived at the plains skip.

It was during the middle of the summer. The Bai Harditts had made the all-night trip by monorail, accompanied by a small donkey—a pet of Maddi's—and crates of chickens. These were taken up to the roof by freight elevator. The guest apartment was opened, the shrine turned to face the wall, and the joss sticks in their jars replaced by marigolds. All of a sudden the sacred room was full of bedrolls, knapsacks, and the small babies of the country Harditts, and looked like a camp.

The younger Harditt children were perched at the window. Dhillon's chin was pressed against a hair braid of his sister Maddi's.

"There's the canal. Look, to the right. There's the synerg, it's blinking. And there's a boat coming."

Maddi said: "What a racket there is. Every time you come to the city they're putting something up or tearing it down." As if to punctuate this remark the sound of riveting came at them from across the plaza.

Not only the city had changed. The Bai Harditts found the fortunes of their city relatives had bettered in recent years. They were more prosperous, for one thing. Olga's own children had grown up, and her daughters had brought back husbands into the compound—from country villages near Sawna. One was a barge pilot and made good money. Another was a tanner.

A grandson, Bangi, was already Srikant's age. Soon Bangi would be coming to Sawna to spend his farm year working for the agricultural collective and living with the Bai Harditts, while Srikant lived at Grain of Millet and learned glass-making.

As a smaller boy Srikant had collected snakes. Now he immersed himself in a book on astrology. He was always looking up references in this to tell the favorable auspices listed for the day, which he would read off to the other children in a pedantic manner. Bangi, who remembered being taken in the village into holes and caves, and the lure of danger, considered his cousin to have become less interesting.

The Bai Harditt children did not consider themselves strangers in the Sixth Ward. But Bangi knew his way around the whole city down to the last alley. He took them to lurid districts and even showed them how to smoke "bhang." He had become a hardened street urchin.

They enjoyed taking the vaporetto. Maddi could spend all day just sitting at the rail eating popcorn. Dhillon collected Karst coins, which he jangled in his pockets.

They also explored the albino sections. Bangi had a friend, Kao, who lived in a Karst dormitory. When they went there, the Sawna children stood still and marveled at everything. Bangi's friend's mother called Maddi "Eyes-as-Big-as-Saucers."

Maddi preferred these excursions with the boys. However, mostly she accompanied her women relatives shopping. On these trips through the crowded streets the older Jat women wore purdah, putting Maddi in agonies of embarrassment. Both her mother and Helvetia wore the long woven shawls up to their noses and seemed to think it perfectly natural, and even Tatti Olga. But Maddi's Aunt Nanda did not wear it.

The family of Jat women commented shamelessly on the Karst women's clothes. Helvetia thought the standard uniform of pants and sleeveless jackets was simply ugly, while Nanda said, "They all looked middle-aged."

To Maddi the Karst women seemed attractive, with their saucy mouths and round transparent faces. She also became conscious of her own neck, which seemed overly long and fragile. She walked down the street carefully, as if balancing her head.

• • •

One day the children walked by a canal. There were the three boys and Bangi's friend from the Noodlemakers, Kao. Bangi was in the lead and very much in charge. Maddi trailed, a burden.

"Hurry up, Maddi."

The sun filtered through a bright haze.

Dhillon and Srikant were throwing rocks at street signs. Each time they hit a sign it went ping...the steel post vibrated. It was like striking a tuning fork, Srikant said. A pleasant crowd was hanging around the dock where the swan boats came in.

Bangi vetoed the suggestion that they take a boat ride to the Spray Farm. Dhillon echoed him: "It's too far. And besides, we've been there before." Bangi and Kao had their own plans.

A Drune family from the Wilderness was having its picture taken on a wooden donkey.

The paths branched off from the embankment. They took one, Dhillon and Kao stopping to chuck stones. They tried hitting further and further signs.

They were walking beside a long fence. Through a hole some children came out carrying boards.

"They're stealing wood for the Fire Festival," Bangi told them. At the same time he held up his hand.

Kao said soberly: "We'll go in. But be careful. Watch out for cops."

On the other side of the fence were old-fashioned row houses sandwiched in between the Points. The houses had wooden back porches, stacked one above the other. At the bottom was a back garden and laundry yard.

Some smaller children stood back. They had been placed as sentinels, their eyes out for trouble on the upper porches. A gang of boys was violently attacking the lower back porch. They had the steps and the railings off already, ripping and twisting and making a ferocious cracking. Then one wrecker would hand a board to waiting helpers.

Bangi and Kao joined the wreckers. Dhillon was about to but his older brother stopped him.

Bangi shouted back: "Oh, it's allowed—the two weeks before Holi. They just pretend it isn't. But don't let anyone see you."

In fact, faces were peering out from the windows of several of the row houses.

Below the wrecking continued. A line of children streamed toward the fence hole with armfuls of boards. On the street they met gangs of other children loaded in the same way, all headed for Franklin Park.

When they got there they found the great Fire Pole set up—which would be used for the Fourth of July Holi pyre. Already there were mountains of wood and rubbish stacked around the base.

ALVAREZ' THIRD LETTER:
THE NOODLEMAKERS

Dawn-Is-Red Superblock
Eighth Ward, Garh
6 Magh

The People's Voice
9 Rockefeller Plaza
New York, N. Y.

Compañeros:
    Things have been going fast. I am now a full-fledged production worker in the Bang Collective. But things haven't been going so well in my domestic life. Of that, more later.
    The Bang artel are noodlemakers. That is what we do. And that is where we go after we leave our communal pod after breakfast—all sixteen pairs of us, our Big Family/Little Family unit.
    I'm told that in past years our artel has done a variety of jobs: vegetable freezing, production of pork sausages, pastry-making...and now noodles. Our members put their whole heart in it and go off to work with great zeal. The other day I marched with a woman seventy years old who sang work songs and strode with a sprightly step. She said: "I have been kept young by cooking."
    I have been working at the noodle factory for several months. I've written you the Karst syndicalist slogan here: "Beyond Socialism." Could this represent a step backward?
    Noodlemakers in Garh: a huge operation, the citizens are crazy about noodles. Our pasta plant is operated with a big flour mill and food producers' co-operative. Very active and aggressive outfit: but can you imagine, they shut down every afternoon! There are about four to five hundred people in our brigade at Checkered Foods, with daily noodle production of

about eighty tons. The various jobs are broken down by sections, as follows:

Egg gathering detail brings in four hundred dozen eggs by trolley from the Spray Farm.

Warehousing. In a warehouse near the mill bags of flour are stored, and brought over by fork-lift.

The "cooks." This detail does mixing and batching, then rolling out the dough. Then the noodles are cut.

Finally the pasta is hung out on racks to dry. After drying it is put into baskets and taken directly to the ward free markets.

It didn't take me long on the job to understand that production is targeted extremely low. Obviously because the operations are too broken up...everything on the scale of a half dozen to a dozen people. Production is all dispersed. It was not hard to see for instance that the warehousing could be combined with the mixing and batching operation—by having a conveyor belt bring the flour directly from the mill and having it come through the dryers and mixers to the vats.

The production plan—arrived at by such an admirable process of democratic centralism in the plant assembly—could be *doubled*!

Of course we have our own self-criticism and work-study sessions in the artel. I was quick to point out the deficiencies of the plan and that with streamlining and efficiency, production could be enormously increased: They only said: "But why?"

However, I have persisted, against resistance. Rebuffed at home, I continue to agitate in my own work section (the warehouse). We have a small nucleus of like-minded persons, call ourselves the Output Group, and distribute handbills.

Unfortunately Kikan, who operates a fork-lift, would be displaced under these reforms.

The older day a "big character poster" attacking us was pasted on the warehouse wall and discussed all day by excited workers. And at home I find myself less popular than before—despite their claims to proletarian internationalism.

But let us advance without compromise! Avanzar sin transar!

I have been having trouble with Kikan. Is it the cigars? which she labels subproletarian and a retrograde nationalist fetish. I am more than ever determined *not* to give up smoking. She has also been after me—and the rest of the sixteens likewise—to bleach my mustache with peroxide.

Kikan has moved to another cubicle.

I am involved in a ferocious ideological dispute with the food producers. I can see now, this simple proposition of mine: the rearrangement of equipment along rational lines, involves serious questions. It seems that the *cooks* (who would also be eliminated under my scheme) enjoy flavoring their own noodles "to the taste": that is, adding spinach, parsley, scallions, certain herbs such as tarragon, etc. It turns out that this "taste" is not for their own palates (in which case it would be a simple issue of civil rights)—but for the marginal differentiation of the product, i.e., for commerce. Each artel *sells* its noodles on the free market to its particular customers who "like their noodles that way."

In other words, they *compete*.

I asked Kikan: Is this Socialism? In turn I am accused of Left Infantilism!

Yours in struggle,

Santiago Alvarez

ALVAREZ' FOURTH LETTER

Dawn-Is-Red Superblock
Eighth Ward, Garh
4 Phagun

Compañeros:

I have attempted during my stay here to "become the new man." I had hoped some day to give you an insider's view of a self-criticism or "struggle" session. Now I am the target of the struggle.

Positions at the plant have hardened during the last month. Big character posters have bloomed against us! Well, they do not accuse me personally..."an unnamed foreigner who is subverting Karst revolutionary methods...and leading us along the road to adventurism." A modest text is labeled "dangerous" that we circulated at our work-study group meetings. "The text is based on none other than Marx's "Critique of the Gotha Programme"!

We are now labeled the "Adventurists" (the Output Group). Kikan's faction—of which she is the head—is called sententiously the "Six-Sides-in-Balance."

Today the dispute came to a head inside our artel—in the most sinister manner, as you can judge for yourselves.

The after-breakfast meeting began with the reading of a sacred text (by Mazda), then a discussion on heat in relation to body movement within the factory. A song praising the First Law of Thermodynamics (heat conservation). It all seemed abstract, and innocent enough. But the heat was on me.

However, the discussion seemed not to be going anywhere at this point. Leaving my mug of coffee on the table, I went to the bathroom.

I returned. Something had altered in the room, violently. I did not know why. Kikan had moved to the front row of the assembled breakfasters where she was painting her nails furiously. My supporters were lined up in front.

They were being forced to give an account of themselves—and when I say forced, I mean the noodlemakers were doing it with relish. As they made their confessions my supporters shifted their feet and avoided looking at me.

Having regained my seat, I sat sipping my coffee and trying to eat my bun, but my heart wasn't in it. The crowd was hostile. At any moment I would be called upon to make my own "auto-criticism."

This would not be difficult. I could see, from the political events of the last weeks, where the land lay.

But what if I committed some *personal* crime?

Kikan looked particularly outraged. The thought occurred to me that while I was out of the room, she had accused me of certain sexual offenses. Perhaps I had not been fornicating in the national style!

I stood before them a foreigner. I looked around the room at this set of uniformly unpigmented complexions and insipid hair and felt suddenly the *blackness* of my mustache. My own face seemed *coarse*, like an overgrown strawberry.

Luckily, as it turned out, this was not to be a trial of un-natural offenses. My case was helped by Big Bang. He spoke in-dulgently on the subject of my ideological shortcomings. I had not "taken the correct line"—but I had tried hard to reform myself, although my background was against me.

A cook seized the floor. He shouted at me:

"You've been running around having a good time and sticking your nose in everything...you don't seem to realize there are crimes in Altai. I can assure you the people are quite able to decide what the crimes are in their own courts and to mete out the appropriate punishment."

The cook's reference to "nosing around" horrified me. I had heard about punishments inflicted by these peoples' courts. One comrade had gotten a hand cut off for pilfering. Another offender, for "meddling," had had his nose slit and been exiled.

I was in a state to expect something of this kind in my own case.

But Big Bang pleaded for leniency because of "special considerations," and suggested in any case this judgment should not be given by the sixteens but by a wider group of neighbors.

And so the sentencing has been postponed.

What I had been found guilty of was "Productionism"—a capital offense—and for certain grave misdemeanors which involved antisocial behavior and "going against harmony."

But I expect the worst.

Fraternally,

Santiago Alvarez

MORRIS' AFTERNOON ON THE NETS

Everything here is refreshing. In the course of my wanderings I keep noting fresh facts. The arts: there seems to be no split between what we would call "commercial arts" and "Art." Nothing is handmade (it's straight from the factory). But everything is, in some personal way, embellished. Thus, somewhat the feeling of "folk art."

• •

Have been interested in locating a small shop where I could set up weaving or chairmaking. Not that I'm eager to make chairs (a tedious business). But I am eager to experience what it's like being associated with one factory as it exists *among others*. In other words, a whole new social system. So that anarcho-syndicalism becomes, in a sense, a fresh background.

• •

A friend has referred me to the Commerce Department. They have put at my disposal an excellent gentleman by the name of Yao Wen-yuan. We have toured the city several times together.

I showed Yao a picture of my famous Morris Chair. He thought it "very pretty" and asked how it was used.

• •

It turns out that in Ngshi-Altai looking for a factory is not so much a question of real estate. Mr. Yao's first questions to me were: with what forms of energy would I want the chair produced? Solar, water power, geothermal, waste products, etc.

And on this depends what brotherhood (groups of artels) I am to seek out in order to make the chair! So already we are a far cry from just going out after available rental space and a work force. (Of course, the basics are the same.)

Looking for a suitable artel (in the solar energy field) we have toured the Eighth Ward extensively.

• •

Answers to mysteries come in a rush.

I had wondered about these small groups of Garhians working around the city. For instance, I spent an afternoon in a park

57

pleasurably watching what I took to be a gang of municipal employees. They were laying out a bed of tulips in the approved manner that must be the same the world over. A battered truck with topsoil...workmen in muddy boots and with spades, and a foreman....

In another case a gang in the streets was repairing a pipe...as office workers watched during the lunch break. But these were not crews of the Department of Parks nor the Department of Public Works, but ordinary (private) artels "spending the afternoon publicly."

Again distinctions break down!

On any afternoon one sees these bands of private citizens out working for the city with a certain air of festivity. Apparently this municipal work is equated with sports—another urban enthusiasm. Now it is summer; but what about the winter, with its icy blasts?

• •

Yao is amused at my notion that public work is done for sport. No, it is labor—but without pay. It is considered a direct exchange between producers, the artels of each community helping each according to need.

I ask, "Are there no wages then in Garh?"

Yao Wen-yuan replies cryptically, "Yes. Socialist in the morning. Communist in the afternoon. And capitalist at odd moments, when there is money to be made."

• •

Yao Wen-yuan has taken me to the area of the nets—the upper membrane above the city where solar energy is trapped. He thinks I might find here some artel suitable for chairmaking. But he is vague on this point.

We are going to spend the afternoon with the "moss-gatherers."

As we rise up from one of the higher levels of our own ward, the whole city comes into view.

This is not one of the ordinary passenger elevators servicing the point houses. The shaft runs vertically up beside an enormous steel tube about twenty feet in diameter—the function of which I am to understand later. At certain points on this tube are "nodes" or branch stations where, Yao Wen-yuan explains, certain small industries are located. Here the passenger elevator also stops.

Apparently we are in an industrial sector.

At the top the view is quite breathtaking. Bright sun... whereas on the levels below there is generally a patchwork effect of light and shade—one of the drawbacks of this "miniaturized" city, one always looks up through layers, either structural parts or membrane. But issuing from the top of the mast one is struck by the bright sky. The first impulse is to shield the eyes.

But of course: on this uppermost layer solar energy is generated.

• •

The highest station. You can imagine being at the top of the pole of a giant circus tent. There is an opening around the pole...the wire cables stretching out...a walkway. Then the immense surface begins, like a shining meadow. At a further distance out, suspended on this meadow, Yao Wen-yuan points out to me a gang of moss-gatherers at work.

This field is a warped plane of hills and hollows, divided along the lines of the supporting tension cables. Along these great catenaries are the promenades. On either side stretches the surface, this *membrane* of sun-absorbing crystals. Making our way, suspended on this floating meadow, we clamber toward these Liliputians. I am introduced to them and we chat for a few moments, as the solar energy-gathering process is explained to me.

• •

Basic energy formulations for solar batteries: a constant of 1.94 calories per minute of sun's heat equals 130 milliwats per centimeter squared. At 10 per cent efficiency this yields 100 watts per square meter of solar batteries at earth's surface.

For continuous supply of energy (regardless of weather conditions) excess solar radiation is taken to energy accumulator/storage batteries.

Solar battery grid at the surface is thin film polycrystalline (silicon or other) layer which absorbs photons, acting as photovoltaic cell.

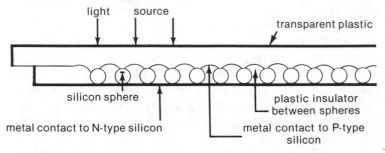

In this way light energy is converted to electrical energy and a simple circuit is set up (generating 100 watts per square meter per minute).

• •

Interesting to note that this constant (the proportion of heat to radiated area of the semiconducting film) is the same as that produced by sunlight falling on a leaf.

Both the leaf and the membrane function as photovoltaic cells: little factories where E (energy) is produced/accumulated, and from which it is taken off to serve life-support functions.

From the cathode layer (see above diagram) current goes to an accumulator and thence to an electrolyzer, where it is stored as gas.

Yao Wen-yuan had wandered off. This was all explained to me by a child.

• •

Yao Wen-yuan and I had approached the small band of thirty to forty persons. I had noticed they were making sweeping movements. Their bodies moving together in rhythm, a band of sweepers covers one section of photolenses at a time. They work downhill, one section of cells at a time. As they work they sway slightly. This process is repeated over and over. From the catenaries they reach over with a long bamboo brush to which a water hose is attached, and lightly wash down the cells (like reaching over and weeding a vegetable patch). The stream of water flushes off the soot and dust that accumulates on the surface of the cells. This is why these afternoon work gangs are called colloquially "moss-gatherers."

The soot and the dust—so they have told me—has drifted on the high air currents from "America."

● ●

A dizzying feeling looking *down* through layers of these sun-trapping stratifications—at the city roofs. Still further down, city squares. Tiny figures are seen threading across a park.

● ●

The moss-gathering section sways up and down gently on its scintillating net. They balance. Again the feeling of a circus performance. I am reminded for some reason of Picasso's picture *Les Saltimbanques.*

● ●

Curiously enough, I am now informed by Yao that this *is* an artel of Singers and Acrobats. In fact they are the very group that we saw performing so profitably in the square before Red Cats. In the evenings they perform commercially; now they are doing their public works exercise.

The sky reflected from the photocells onto these albino faces—makes them bright blue. But the figures are cheerful. They chatter and hop around like so many sparrows, hardly bothering to look down.

I chat with the Red Cats acrobat who was sitting beside me in the speak-chamber, and she tells me her impression of the Assembly. She says that the "dancers are getting old and clumsy."

● ●

From the solar membrane covering the city with its millions and millions of photocells, the electrical energy accumulates at the poles.

At the tops of each pole there is an electrolyzer station. Here water is disassociated by the solar current into its component gases. The gases (in the form of hydrogen and oxygen gas) are then stored in the pipe cylinders. These are called "tank farms."

The tank farms also function as the power-distributing system. At lower stations on the pole the electrolysis process is reversed: water is reformed and the recombination of the gases produces current for the industrial power outlets.

Here is the quantitative electrolysis formula:

1. Solar batteries ⟶ E accumulator ⟶ electrolyzer
2. Water disassociated to two parts (17 cu. ft.) hydrogen and one part (8.5 cu. ft.) oxygen volume, and compressed to 100 atmospheres
3. Fuel cell: reaction is reverse electrolysis
   H_2 (g) + O (g) ⟶ H_2O
   yields 56.6 kilocalorie/mole = 1.23 volts

• •

We are not dealing here with large amounts of energy. The solar energy available to the whole of the Eighth Ward would be less than that delivered by several large plants using coal or hydropower. But the method of storage and delivery of the power is novel.

Four hundred and twenty gallons of water produces one kilowatt per hour electricity for use, the tank farm delivering on the order of two to five hundred thousand gallons to each point. Thus each reverse-electrolyzer station at one of the system's nodes has clustered around it a number of small- to medium-sized manufacturing plants.

• •

Another tree analogy: As the photocells function as the canopy of leaves, these enormous tubes rising everywhere throughout Garh are the trunks containing the transport and nutrient system (corresponding to the phloem and xylem tubes of the tree).

Perhaps this is not merely a metaphor. What a simple system: yet somehow miraculous.

Indeed, what could be more natural: that the basic design system of a city should be that of a forest?

In Garh, each borough owns, and is composed of, its "tree trunks" (direct sources of power).

• •

Another question. I've been told the city is divided into ten wards. Is the whole city then decentralized in this way, i.e. do the separate power sources (photoelectrical, steam, etc.) guarantee the political autonomy of each ward?

If so, what is the federating principle?

Possibly there may be no Garh City in the sense of a physical entity. The "city" may be merely an aesthetic impression. (I am reminded of the synerg from its great tower winking its municipal data as we arrived.)

A metropolitan illusion?

CRYSTAL GROWING/AN
ANARCHIST BUREAUCRACY

Yao has found me a manufacturer. However, the product manufactured will not be chairs. As it turns out chairs are not used in Nghsi—people squat on the floor on mats. I had gotten the wrong impression from Intourist, and Yao had been too much of a diplomat to tell me. In fact when I had shown him a picture of my Morris Chair he had not known what it was.

But the designs for fabrics and the famous Morris flower patterns on drapes and wallpapers offer distinct commercial possibilities here. And so I have made up a portfolio, including some of Blake's fanciful engravings which have an art nouveau flare.

It is this portfolio which Yao has been taking around.

So now we have a prospective client that Yao tells us is "a dynamic outfit." We have an appointment with their Research and Development section.

• •

This morning we have come for our appointment with the Crystal Growers, at the very top of one of the big office buildings. The appointment is with the chief engineer of this artel. We wait in the reception room. An exhibit showing the development of the firm is explained to us by a young technician.

Like so many of the solar industries located at the nodes the fortunes of this one have grown with technological advances in energy-gathering. The old sunlight absorption surface had been composed of millions of individual photocells, each a single silicon seed crystal one by two centimeters in diameter embedded in a matrix. The artel has developed a thin polycrystalline film which can be rolled out in a single layer. This is more flexible, and vastly more economical.

However, the absorption properties, the technician explains, are the same: depending on the material, the photons must be absorbed with enough energy to bridge the band gap.

The artel, after experimenting with a number of new materials, including a "light" silicon, Indian phosphide and silenium, finally hit upon "gallium," a workable composite which could be spun out in a continuous mat like fiberglass.

This material is melted and poured over a plate. In the process of cooling there is a deposition of dendrite crystals.

Yao and I are given the opportunity to examine one of these lovely crystals under a microscope—also a feature of this stylish exhibit.

The Crystal Growers have gone into the domestic home products market. They make a number of items: "thin film" carpeting and wallpaper, insulating material, crystal radio sets, a small solar generating panel for commune laundries—in addition to fabrics and certain applications of engraving.

Our wait for the Research and Development head turns out to be long. I begin to get impatient, but we are told this prominent official "is in the legal department" of the artel overseeing the draft of our contract and that "she is anxious to meet us."

Concentrating on the scientific exhibit I had not noticed how impressively decorated the reception room is. It is in the grand style, with oak-paneled walls and several dignified, bluff oil portraits in gold frames. Could these be of the founders?

But finally we are shown in. Vigorous words of greeting from across the room and a broad smile. We are introduced. I remember with surprise that I have seen the face on television. It is Mrs. Zowie.

However, she does not have on her fatigue cap, the badge of political authority from the stadium. She wears instead the large bonnet of the guild master decorated with plastic cherries.

• •

I wonder if I should pay Yao Wen-yuan a finder's fee? In fact there are all sorts of uncertainties having to do with getting our designs manufactured by the Crystal Growers. For instance, must Blake and I live with this artel in one of their dormitories now that we are production partners? That is the law here. But Mrs. Zowie has advised us that "we can get around it somehow."

What about patents, royalties, etc.? How is this to be managed? And what about the contract between ourselves, that is Blake and myself, and the artel—since individuals are not recognized as legal entities here? Contracts are only made between collectives.

In this regard too Yao tells us that Mrs. Zowie "has arranged everything."

• •

I had not visited Yao's office before. I found it on the second floor of the Flatbush National Bank Building, the same that houses the Crystal Growers (in the penthouse). If you will believe it, the mint, where they print their own currency, is also located here.

I had noticed the many varieties of money in use in Garh. Each ward—even each borough—has its own currency, which is exchanged somehow. Horrible thought: could they be intending to use our designs—or more exactly, Blake's engravings—to manufacture bank notes?

I decide to keep this possibility to myself.

In his office Yao is depressed, says he has a head cold and can hardly breathe. He complains of the paper work.

"In the old days it wasn't so much. Now there are carloads of it. We are strangled in red tape."

I tell him that with the elimination of printing in Nghsi I would have expected the elimination of paper work.

Yao sighs and says: "The documents have to be preserved for legal reasons." He refers to the commercial agreements between the artels, deeds of leasing, licensing of patents, etc.

Upon stepping off the elevator I had reached Yao's section down a decayed marbled corridor. A reception desk. The office occupies the entire floor, which is divided into cubicles. In each one, blurred by frosted glass, some applicant was being interviewed for a license.

Sniffling through his nose, Yao is constantly on the telephone with Mrs. Zowie.

On the wall of Yao's cubicle is a photograph of the chairman of his department.

It would seem that bureaucracies are the same the world over.

•   •

We are at the Red Cats again and meet up with old friends. Lin Piao of the steelworkers' syndicate has dropped by. He is a friend of Bang's. Bang, the veteran faction chief, has recovered from his exhausting performance at the Assembly. And Yao Wen-yuan has recovered from his cold.

But Yao is habitually depressed. His head droops over the table. He has been drawing his finger listlessly through a puddle of beer.

The Commons will not meet tonight over its multicom. It is an ordinary evening at the Red Cats, of food and acrobatics.

I am wondering out loud: Are there rich and poor in Garh? I have seen no poor people—only poor sections of the city, relatively.

"Yes. Some boroughs, even whole wards are rich," Lin Piao admits. "How can one avoid it? Some artel makes an invention. Associations are formed. Inevitably this leads to the accumulation of wealth, and to power."

We discuss the Crystal Growers. Bang explains that, expanding their polycrystalline lines, they controlled numerous power outlets at the nodes. Recently they had gone into mining.

"There's plenty of gallium. In the petrified forest, near Zimbabwe. They have a complete monopoly." Lin Piao is cynical. Mrs. Zowie, he says, was now a member of the Solar Producers Board. The Crystal Growers sponsored one of the "dance houses" and several of their officers had become long-term senators of the Rotary Club.

I had thought this was illegal.

"It's true. All positions in the Rotary Club are impermanent. But some are less impermanent than others."

Bang calls for more beer and sausages.

I tell them I would like to explain my "medieval theory" of capital accumulation in Garh.

Briefly, the theory is this: that Garh and presumably the other cities of the Rift—are at a precapitalist stage. That is, economic activity is generated by the guilds (the artels) and tied to a limited free market. As it was in the cities of Antwerp or Bruges in the late Middle Ages in Europe.

Of course, there are differences. For instance the improvements in solar technology by the Crystal Growers do not make them the "owners" of the technology in the same way that a group of Flemish merchants would be the owners, say, of a fulling mill.

But, somehow benefits accrue. This is due to licensing agreements, patents, etc.

There were also the religious attitudes. In Altai the stress is on the communal, on the brotherhood bonds. In the Europe of the late Middle Ages the individual was not so important either:

66

it was the guild of artisans. But this was weakening even at that time. The character of the entrepreneur was changing.

I mention certain medieval works of art of which I am particularly fond: the biographies of adventurers by Froissart and the sharp character portraits of Holbein. In the eyes of these merchant princes and guilds craftsmen, as they sit with their tools and counting boxes around them, one can see the future history of Europe.

I felt the same thing ahead for Nghsi—I tell my companions—as I looked into Mrs. Zowie's eyes.

Yao continues drawing disconsolately in his beer puddle.

Bang denies that they are in a state of precapitalist accumulation: "No, no. That's all behind us, centuries ago. What do you think is the meaning of our slogan: 'Beyond Socialism'?"

He admits on the other hand that people did tend to backslide. There had to be "periodic rectification campaigns."

Lin Piao looks at me gravely. He says: "And it is extraordinary to look at Nghsi-Altai through *your* eyes."

Suddenly from outside the Commons there is a squawl of martial music. Yao lifts up his head. Everyone is at the window of the burghall. There is a band of bagpipers marching down the street.

"The mummers' parade," someone exclaims. "Next week will be the Fourth!"

A chain of small explosions, which they say are from gas bombs, shakes the Red Cats window. Outside a crowd of panhandlers seems to have descended on the little square. They are dressed in rags and hold out their bowls piteously.

"They are from the Tenth Ward," Yao remarks with great satisfaction. "They are practicing begging."

PATRIOTIC PAGEANTRY/
CHILDREN'S GAMES

The Minutemen are going down the street. Long ago people have forgot what their uniforms mean. It is only known: "In a moment they were able to mobilize." Against what?

The Adversary lost in time.

The alert of the drums, the shrill of the fifes now calls us—to pleasure. Under his snapping anarchist banner, my son stands selling pretzels.

●   ●

We will become the Rooster Dancers, also called The Alarmists, because these roosters which sit so placidly on our shoulders were in fact once alarm clocks. There's no mistaking the roosters' colors: their fiery red and their fierce black is of—NOW. I pluck a tailfeather for decoration.

Soon all these alarm clocks will go off, calling us from sleep. And to action around the Fire Pole.

●   ●

Legendary heroes, a brigade of SQUATTERS marches by to struggle against the HARD HATS. Their emblem is corrugated tin. And these wire cutters, crowbars, jimmies and oxyacetylene torches are their keys of office. The old fences are down. From the tin sheets they will resurrect Resurrection City.

But this battle has been won years ago.

●   ●

We will join you on this, the fifth day of the festival which is to last fourteen days, to eat "fire crackers." And "gulgulas," patriotic pancakes, which were perhaps originally made with red pepper.

●   ●

Tangles of barbed wire. Clippers are used to cut into the currency exchanges and luxury hotels of El Centro—the international hotel section. Their bronze doorknobs are now preserved in museums.

●   ●

68

An effigy of the chairman of the board of the last historically recorded Steel Co-ordinating Committee is burned, by the so-called Blue Man.

●   ●

Overlays of legend, one obscuring the other.

●   ●

Now every low dive is emptied and from the poolrooms and sports palaces erupt whole squadrons of HARD HATS who rush in the direction of Franklin Park. They are members of the syndicates on their day off.

To the defense of the Tenth Ward! And ancient codes.

They go by with a dazzling display of technical apparel. From our shoulders the roosters taunt them.

●   ●

So on this day of the year only "gas" is sold.

●   ●

The traditional "gas dragons" one hundred feet in the air, of inflated rubber, are loose! Breathing their nostalgic fumes. The gas dragon has ten tails made out of colored paper. Cut each tail off in turn, hordes of squatters and "swamp alligators," future citizens, will erupt violently.

●   ●

They are called milliliters: these small bombs consisting of milliliter cans of gas which are thrown by the children of squatters under the motorcycles of the National Planners.

●   ●

And what do they hold up, these raiders and these revelers? Weeds flowering on the back lots.

●   ●

Remember your origins, you most honorary and respected of the Syndicate Leaders, in these clandestine squatters organizations. Wear rags of every color! Put on your "rooster finery."

CHILDREN'S GAMES OF THE TEN-FOURTH

Here is a song / game / dance performed with foreign word borrowings while making mud pies, supposedly on a stove. The "pies" are made and served.

Q. Children, what would you like to eat today?

A. Roast Beef. Roast Beef...with Pittsburg sauce.

Q. Children, children, what would you like to eat next?

A. Lamb chops, with Chicago gravy.

Q. Children, then what do you want?

A. Oysters Rockefeller.

Then all the pies are dropped and squashed up. On top of the pile is planted a stalk of joe-pye weed.

• •

Marching on to the National Capital

All children take their "automobiles." When the children arrive at the Capital, they give food to the "starving" congressmen.

(This pantomime is from the National Famine era.)

• •

Stock Villains of Puppet Shows

Stompers-Gompers, the Centralizer. The children stuff pennies into his pockets. Another: Uncle Fatso.

• •

Piñata Game

A "trailer truck" made of pâpier-maché is hung up. It is filled with elaborately wrapped packages in containers, plastic bags, etc. The truck is destroyed with canes of bamboo.

BLAKE IN THE WILDERNESS

At Egwegnu University the students had departed. The lake was vacant—none of the little sanjhi boats with their fluttering candles that the children had thrown stones at on the night of the Lights Festival. The dormitories had been cleaned out and dusted. It was the term's end.

Tutuola and Blake left for a walking trip through the woods to visit some holy places.

They carried nothing but the clothes on their backs, a couple of woven straw ponchos, a Coleman stove, and a rucksack.

The forest fascinated Blake. But soon he grew tired of it. The lonely footfalls on the path went on endlessly. The monkeys chattered in the murky canopy. They waded through deep moss during the day and at night rested against trees twined with orchids.

The path was well used. Wood deer traveled that way. A family of zemboks joined the pilgrims for a stretch of the journey, the buck with his great boss and striped hide, walking with slow stride several paces ahead, the cubs frolicking to the side out in the bush. That night Blake lay down in his coat and dreamed of huge lions with the face of God.

They visited several shrines, at which both men worshiped and left bowls of meal. Blake had taken a slight chill which developed into a chest cold by morning. Tutuola kept the fire going continually, wrapped him in both ponchos, and fed him tea brewed from roots. They were by a peat bog. They talked far into the night. The blue shaman asked Blake to tell him something about his birthplace.

Blake's account of the City of London:

"London where I saw the light of day in 1757 was a city of half a million people, and grew in the next fifty years to one million. My father was a hosier. I was born above his shop on Broad Street in the parish of Marylebone.

"The first sounds in my ear were the wagons of the carters clattering over the cobbles. As a small boy I was in and out of the wheels, while the carters cursed. We oversaw with pleasure the unloading of casks and bales. In the winter I could watch the lamps being lit in the gloom. Our town London was notable in the Europe of that time for its improved streets and street services. We had covered sewers, a novelty. I can well remember a gang of men digging a sewer along Aldermaston Street. I marveled at how they threw up the gravel. We followed them a stretch each day for the five months they worked—and in that way came upon the Thames.

"I think that was the first time, also, I saw the sky.

"We were very cramped. The city had pushed out beyond us years before—to Saint Giles, Cottage Terrace, King's Crown, St. Pancras. New subdivisions, new factories as well. My whole horizon was the buildings, with our church piercing one edge of the skyline, and Big Ben another. Those bells had a dead sound. Nearby there was an alehouse; and that was full of light, talkers, and smoke on a winter's night—much more cheerful than the church.

"You may remember my lines: 'Dear mother, dear mother, the church is cold,/But the Ale-house is healthy and pleasant and warm.'"

Tutuola asked: "So the country was far away in your London?"

Blake: "I don't remember seeing a blade of grass or a weed till I was fifteen and my mother took me to St. Pancras. I couldn't have named you any bird but a cheeping sparrow though I was a great expert on market fowl and the crawfish and crabs they trundled from door to door. I could never write in the country. After a few months in the fresh air composing lyrics about sunflowers I was in a rage to get back."

Tutuola: "What was the weather like?"

Blake: "Clammy and wet. Horrible. The worst weather in the world. A grim place. The closed courts, the tenements Dickens describes. Tuberculosis. I'll tell you, the average Londoner didn't live long. It was a life-and-death matter when you sent the bucket out, and the children returned with a few lumps of soft coal."

Tutuola: "You spoke of the chimney sweeps."

Blake: "I knew several. Tom Dacre was one, whose sister was a whore. How extraordinary those poor fellows looked with their stove hats and faces covered with grime. It was a marvel to watch them climb out of a chimney. I don't wonder I was struck by it and took them in my writing as messengers from another world.

"And Tom's sister—standing on an icy corner in her finery against the stones of some bank... A face printed in hell.

"Scenes. Scenes. Hogarth was the painter. Rowlandson... Yes, yes. There it was bitter weather."

The Deodar asked him: "I suppose you've seen the notebooks of Hiroshige? The Tokyo of his time—twice as large as London and Paris combined. His sketches are fascinating."

Blake: "Yes, but I never drew from the visible world. The human figure yes, that was from life and taken directly after Michelangelo and the Greeks. But the *world* in which they moved was phantasmagoric. Good God, as if there would have been any point in *describing* London. No. The spiritual world was all my aim.

"But I am a great admirer of Hiroshige. He scribbled some verses too."

●　●

They had another discussion in which Blake questioned Tutuola on the priesthood's practice of celibacy. His answer (unsatisfactory to Blake) was "the animals are in the forest, from which we draw our strength." And added that the relationship helped "restore balance."

Sexual satisfaction from animals the shaman seemed to take matter-of-factly. He was far more interested in London and returned to that subject. Tutuola asked:

"So the city was so large you say you could scarcely conceive the end of it?"

Blake: "I could scarcely. In my mind it went on forever. And beyond it another world which I called Paradise."

"The city kept growing?"

Blake: "Buildings, churches, warehouses, factories which produced as much steel and cloth as Birmingham and Manchester—a smoky pall which ate up the countryside round about as well.''

Tutuola quoted the lines:

"There's the dirt and the smoke
and the millworking folk...
Manchester's not a bad town.''

Blake laughed and explained that was the wrong "Manchester.'' The poem referred to another industrial city in "New'' England.

Tutuola: "So England is growing continuously too? Tell me, this fascination for murk and grime. It's not conceivable to you for a city to be clean?''

Blake picked his teeth and did not reply.

"I noticed you spoke of the London of your day using the harshest imagery. Surely it was not the city of the Lamb and the Rose, and 'piping down the valleys wild.' But of something diabolical.''

"But of course!'' Blake cried. "The City is an infernal machine! And the principle of boundless energy.''

"And man is innocent, against the bloody stones?''

"It is true there is a crime against the heart, but that is the price paid for all the power, fire, and light bursting out. The city's image is the open-hearth blast furnace. No, not the Rose...but the ingot turning to rose in the smelter.''

"Even the furnace has to be metered,'' his companion suggested. "This seems a curious notion to me, this energy source which is infinite and expanding. For us the city is not an engine, but subject to organic rhythms. It is not a tree—but a forest of trees. And so should be thinned occasionally.''

"Who is to'thin it?''

"We have a saying here in Nghsi: 'Once in a man's lifetime he watches the city die.' That implies I suppose that the two—the man and the city—are of the same measure.''

• •

The forest was still around them. They had been following a narrow track among the cliffs, unable to ascend or go down.

Tutuola had built a grass hut. They were sitting in a narrow clearing near the base of a waterfall. Crags rose above them. Spume drifted over the small island from the falls. The beads of moisture seemed to weigh down the bamboo. Blake's socks hung on sticks.

The fire kept sputtering from the damp wood and even the smoke appeared heavy. Blake, who had begun to suffer from cold and was wondering when he would ever get his clothes dry, was surprised to hear a whistle blast, followed by the rumble of a train. He thought they might be near one of the lines that carried freight to the forest cantonments, but Tutuola said it was a factory whistle.

There was another blast from below. The sun began to break through, and the mist cleared. In a short time they were looking down at the city of Garh.

"The city is never far away," the priest said. "Either in our imagination or in our experience. The walls of the canyon muffle it. But sometimes, when the wind is right, the noises carry almost to Egwegnu."

It was enough for Blake to look down on Garh, its canals, its towers, the steaming ducts. The wayfarers did not go down. When they broke camp and re-entered the wilderness, Blake felt refreshed.

Tutuola also seemed exhilarated and walked in front of Blake with a light step.

A yellow butterfly settled on the blue priest's beard. He cut a stick of bamboo and carried it.

Then he repeated: "No, the city is never far away. We will re-enter it soon."

THE FIRE FESTIVAL

Yao Wen-yuan heard the cock crow. The noise would be coming from the mummer's band down in the street. It was somewhat earlier than his usual waking hour.

Each dancer attired in holiday costume had a stridently crowing cock on his head. Sometimes a band would actually practice for these performances, or at least learn how to play the instruments correctly. Judging from the sound drifting up from far below, this group was very inept.

Already everyone in the bookkeeping artel was up. They were talking about the Ten-Fourth holiday and greeting each other. "Spreccia!"

"Spreccia!"

Rubbing his eyes Yao went over to the window. Below him on the street the mummers were milling around beating on tin sheets. A small crowd of kids were setting off milliliters, which exploded in ripples.

In the past few days the Eighth Ward had been invaded by mummers. There were two kinds; mummers who were dressed as Squatters, wearing rags of red and orange colors. The others, called Hard Hats, wore black costumes somewhat like old-fashioned policemen. They were called the Red and Black Mummers and appeared on the streets of Garh once every ten years on the Fourth of July holiday.

On that day a special breakfast is served: red cranberry muffins drenched in molasses, like pancakes. These are sometimes called "patriotic pancakes." And the children munch hard biscuits, "fire crackers."

Yao decided he would not go to the office right away but would make a detour along the bank of the canal to see what was happening. As Yao came out of the elevator into the lobby he was accosted by a crowd of rag bedecked squatters. There were also beggars from the Tenth Ward. He recognized some business clients.

Along the canal it was sunny and noisy. It was already jammed with boats, crowding each other and blowing their whistles. When he reached his office in the bank building a half hour later, he found everything in disorder. A young woman clerk in his section stood before a window blowing papers out into the street with an electric fan. The filing cabinet stood open behind her. She was calling gaily to other clerks to watch. Papers in four colors drifted on air and sidled down toward the pavement.

Yao Wen-yuan told her: "You mustn't do that. Those are important files." In spite of himself he was shocked.

"But it's the Fourth!" All the Karst clerks wore bright fingernail polish and their cheeks were rouged. The woman stuck her tongue out at him.

"Well, yes. I suppose so."

Elsewhere the office was a scene of cheerful confusion. Mechanical shredders were in operation eating up files. Duplicate and triplicate papers were being consumed in burn-baskets. Already the place had taken on the air of an office party. Junior clerks were drinking from paper cups. From a cubicle a couple ran into the aisle pulling each others' hair and screaming. Windows were wide open. Yao felt a mixture of horror and relief.

As he went out into the street for the noon hour, another group of employees threw colored powder at him. "Spreccia!" "Spreccia," the head clerk answered.

•   •

Balloons were rising past the Noodlemakers' apartments and catching in the solar net. Each time a balloon came by the windows of the pod, coasting and eddying, infants would scream. All were privileged to be home from the nursery for the Fire holidays.

The faces of the older children were already smeared with powders. The gang had been at work outside on the plaza all morning. Periodically Kao and Bangi, his friend, reappeared for tools. Now they had come for a soldering torch.

They were followed by four country children. The youngest Jat girl, Maddi, sucked at her fire-cracker, which she had smeared with ghi. Kao's sister Peach Blossom was also munching her cracker.

It was the morning when everyone in the superblock was constructing their "Tinguely machines."

"Be careful," Kikan's mother said, brushing aside the boy's hair. "Don't self-destruct."

But of course, that was the point of a Tinguely machine! The children rushed toward the elevator.

"Is it really dangerous?" Srikant asked Bangi as they came out into the courtyard. He did not want to ask the Karst boy.

"Well, is it?" Bangi turned blandly to Kao. But the older boy was busy examining the tip of the soldering torch. He turned the knob a fraction, and compressed air hissed out. They were accompanied by several other Noodlemaker kids. A step or two behind Kao a Karst cousin was carrying a length of cable. Dhillon and Maddi and the smaller Noodlemakers were clutching bags of colored powder.

Each crew in the courtyard had been fabricating its own Tinguely. The large paved space, an extension of the lobbies of several point houses, was full of these enormous constructs. Groups of older onlookers gathered around them with an amused air. The constructs looked flimsy. Most of them had been fitted together with rods, wheels, and bits of sheet metal tenuously held together with wire or solder. Small motors made the parts move. In fact this was what was being tried out now.

Kao started an electric motor, and a bicycle wheel began to revolve. It was geared to a series of larger wheels by belts. A ball descended a chute, and on the top a vane swung around as if pushed by the wind.

Dhillon and Maddi watched for a while, then wandered off. The whole plaza was full of Tinguelys. Some of the models looked like giant birds with elaborate tails and wing structures covered with bright silk. Others were like industrial machines, with gears, greased tracks, and cable drums. Some were spindly and spidery, balanced like dentists' drills.

The country Harditts were wide eyed, and so even was Peach Blossom. Hopping up and down with impatience, she cried: "When does it begin? When?"

At three o'clock all these machines would begin to go off at once. Fantastic nonsense. Explosions. One level of the "self-destruct" contraptions gyrating and collapsing on another level. The prospect thrilled Dhillon.

• •

As the Grain of Millet residents passed through the Sixth Ward they ran into people with shopping carts going in the other direction. The carts were loaded with consumer items.

Olga told them, "They're from Konsum," naming a big department store in the Tenth Ward.

Occasionally the group ran into a crowd of dancers. The mummers no longer carried their roosters. They had been released—perhaps because their function of awakening the town was now over. The roosters had been allowed to fly off, like the balloons.

The country Harditts were astonished at the crowds. They were being pushed helter-skelter. Sathan had to step off the curb so as not to be bumped into by a loaded cart. But in the street they were liable to be run over.

A shopping cart cavorted by harnessed to a goat. Helvetia pointed it out with amusement to the other women. They would probably be Jats. Nanda walked beside Maddi holding her niece by the hand.

There was much throwing of colored powders. As they crossed a square a drunken woman came out of the burghall beating a man with a stick.

This feature of the Fourth was a familiar one to the Sawna women. It was the country way of celebrating.

Helvetia said, "The women are getting their own back."

"Here the women don't have to get their own back. They do what they like," Olga remarked.

Today none of the Jat women was wearing purdah.

They were on a "shopping spree"—an event that occurred not every Fourth of July, but every tenth Fourth. Hence, this festival was called the Ten-Four. They had brought several of their own carts for carrying things. Olga's mother, Sandranapaul, the matriarch of the urban clan, was with them. A woman of seventy, she insisted on pushing a cart—particularly as they passed acquaintances.

Helvetia (who was actually older) kept calling her "Grandmother," much to the other matriarch's annoyance. On this holiday Helvetia was pleased to ask:

"Grandmother, are you sure this is not stealing? Walking halfway across town, and breaking into a department store! The idea."

"It's being torn down anyway," the old woman replied.

Olga's clan took this adventure in stride. The Sawna children were apprehensive. They could hardly believe that they were bound for a "free" zone where rules regarding property were suspended. Maddi kept watching for the police.

In fact at several intersections of the Sixth Ward streets Hard Hats were on patrol. Increasingly they ran into groups of runaways from the destabilized neighborhoods. A stream of refugees passed them. From time to time they met a Drune priest jangling a bell and waving his "wilderness branches."

They were approaching the border between the Sixth and Tenth wards. The pace quickened. The crowds were more packed. They were swept faster. More carts laden with goods were returning. At the same time local people were watching them from the balconies. They kept urging them to move on.

"Not here. Not here. Across the canal!"

They laughed and threw colored powder down. From railings anarchist flags snapped. The shops below were barricaded against the raiders.

The crowd finally swept across the canal bridge into the Tenth. For the first time they could see with their eyes the condition of this ward. It was pitiful. The wreckers had preceded them. Many of the superblocks had already been torn down. Rising from the desolation was the Tenth Ward stadium, which would be the scene of the Fire Pole celebration that evening.

Near the canal bank which they had now reached the department store, Konsum, stood along an open square. It was in the process of being ransacked. Clusters of Hard Hats watched helplessly.

A packed mass of people stood on the sidewalk pressed against the building. All the show windows had been smashed. Heaps of looted furniture and broken counters were being used as steps up into the store. Over these barricades people clambered in and out, handing things down—radios, flamboyant dolls, refrigerators, curtains. These were passed over the heads of the crowd to the back and miraculously secreted in the carts. It didn't seem to matter whether the articles were whole or broken.

• •

The syndicalists had retired to a restaurant on the bank of the canal. Blake and Morris sat with them, drinking beer and watching the demolition as it proceeded. These were members of the Builders and Wreckers Syndicate. Not far from their table on the terrace of the café a steady stream of paraders were going by. Children held balloons.

Across the canal, the boom of a fantastically tall crane moved across the face of one of the point houses. This was one of the syndicate's "nibbling cranes." On a cable hung a clam-shell bucket. In this, two men were suspended like balloonists in a gondola—the cutters. The building mast was constructed in modules held together by rods in tension. Long tubes of oxy-acetylene gas swung in the air, hanging down in loops from the bucket. Delicately the men would lean out into the sky, cut certain of the rods, and a part of the building would fall.

The foreman was explaining to Morris and Blake that the demolition of the buildings was professional. The job was con-tracted out among the syndicates of the ward, bids being taken on an entire superblock. Different artels had different methods. There was a lively spirit of "mutualist competition."

The sky was filled with rigging. Puffs of steam from other cranes drifted over the work site. The foreman explained that as the inhabitants of a superblock became displaced and moved out, that section of the borough came down. That was all there was to it.

They could see across the cleared space all the way to the further canal. There the adjoining ward stood, a diminished skyline. Already several square miles of the Tenth was waste space. Only the ruins of one of the department stores was left and several of the national banks whose solid marble fronts had so far resisted being dismantled.

There was a tremendous explosion. In the near distance a section of a point house shot out sideways into space like a pile of exploding barrels. The top of the structure hung in the air an instant, with its apartments, radio towers, and the booms sup-porting the solar arrays—then wavered. It plunged straight down into the basement, raising a cloud of dust.

"Dynamite," the foreman remarked. He added that he thought this job—which had been done by another artel—was unnecessarily heavy handed.

"What we are observing," Blake remarked with some awe, "is a systematic destruction of one tenth of the city."

• •

"Here they come!"

"Spreccia! Destroy the Tenth!" yelled the small Dhillon, not knowing what the cry meant.

The Bang and Harditt children, separated from the Noodlemakers, were wedged onto the sidewalk behind the barricades. Everyone seemed drunk or camouflaged under streaks of holi powder.

Rooster feathers were stuck in Bangi's hair. The small fry were behind him. Bangi had picked up a pair of wire-clippers somewhere. The children were ragged, Maddi's coat was torn, and Kao's younger brother had lost one of his shoes.

Already they looked like Squatters.

They crawled under the barricade again and rejoined Kikan. After a halt Bang's artel was beginning to straggle into line. Beside them the canal was empty and lurid. There were no boats allowed beyond the Sixth Ward express stop because of danger from skyrockets and falling debris.

Because of the great crowds the marchers were continually having to stop. During these halts, an artel or even a whole section would squat on the boulevard watching the puppet shows. Some of them would go into a café and drink beer or pulque.

Following the Noodlemakers in the line of march was a foreign quarter, the Grain of Millet neighborhood. In this contingent came the other members of the Harditt family. One of Olga's brothers and Venu struggled to hold up a Sawna landscape stretched aloft on bamboo poles.

In the line of march the major syndicates were represented. Most of them had put together elaborate floats, showing the lives of the Great Decentralizers. The Zimbabwe steelworkers came by dragging a float with moving parts operated by steam. The Electrolyte-storage Operators followed. Then, the Recycling Depots. Then, the Honey-bucket Men in gleaming white coveralls accompanying a brigade from the spray farm. The paraders surged past, treading on the pavement thick with the remains of exploded milliliters.

During one of these halts, Maddi, exhausted by the day's happenings, sat down with her smaller brother on the slope of the embankment and began to cry.

The children could barely see across the canal into "Waste Land." The marchers who had already gotten in and crossed the bridges had scattered and were running back and forth under the cranes. On the mountainous piles of rubble, battles were being fought. The children watched the seesawing struggle, at the top the Hard Hats defending, from the base the Squatters surging up with their wire-cutters and blood-curdling shouts.

"Spreccia!"

"Down with the Center!"

There was a blast of bagpipes. Ahead the columns had started up again, but the Noodlemakers were still wedged. To the rear inflated figures soared up in the sky and began to plunge forward.

"The Gas Dragons are coming!"

A flotilla of Gas Dragons, villains and heroes of folk history, soared by over the Noodlemakers' heads. The great figures were held down to earth with wires, but barely. The riggers struggled with them, lurching and bucking as they went along the street straining their necks up.

•   •

By nine o'clock all the banks had been dynamited. The municipal debt moratorium had been declared.

It seemed as though most of the population of Garh had been compressed into Waste Land. The rest were spectators lining the far banks of the canals.

The paraders had entered the grounds, but the parades were over. The skirmishes had been fought. Armies of the night—the black/the red—were scattered with the scattered holi powders.

Small bands from the various neighborhoods kept together, were separated in the crowd and darkness, found each other again.

"Happy Fourth!"

"Spreccia!"

Everyone was converging on the Franklin Park stadium.

In the leveled landscape that had been the Tenth Ward only a few national bank buildings still burned beside great heaps of rubble. The stolid marble walls were torn open. Gutted interiors continued to smolder. A pile of beams would ignite suddenly. Sparks which floated overhead mixed with the fallout of sky-rocket comets.

Venu's arm was around Sathan's waist. She had drawn her shawl around her. Maddi clung to her mother tightly. The child's face was smudged. Her hair, wet from the heat, was plastered against her forehead.

Maddi had been given the slip by the boys, who were already up on the berm of the stadium perhaps. At ten o'clock would begin the burning of the holi pyre.

They had seen Blake move off several minutes before, with a boy (Dhillon?) on his shoulders. Or could it have been Peach Blossom? The child had one hand gripped across Blake's eyes and with the other held up a sparkler. As they waded into the dark crowd, the light from the sparkler could be seen for some time wavering and bobbing.

Then it was lost among other small fires.

A ferris wheel was turning off to the right. A line of exhausted children waited below it in the dark. The wheel went around, and the gondolas as they reached the top were lighted by a glow coming vaguely from inside the berm of the stadium.

Elsewhere in the crowd Tante Olga had been leading the older Harditt women. Helvetia refused to go a step further. The country matriarch's shawl had been trampled. And she had lost a jeweled brooch, an ancestral heirloom.

The women had come to rest along the side of the canal by the steps of a demolished bank. The Sawna matriarch had pulled up her khurtah and was bathing her feet. In the water near them mummers, dressed as "swamp alligators," were still dumping currency into the canal. The sodden notes floated off.

Helvetia, her gums purple with betel nut and her hair in a tangle, spat out:

"What hysteria. Imagine. To replace a whole section of a city like a worn out part!"

The idea struck the old woman as so comical, she promptly revived and got up. She began throwing colored powder at Nanda, shouting and guffawing.

"Energy! Spreccia!"

• •

The landscape below the stadium was like a dark sea. People floundered up through the tall grass and heather of the berm as if up the flank of a great wave.

Bangi and Dhillon were on the promenade of the stadium. The escalators were now closed and guarded. Breaches had been made in the berm by giant earth-movers colored a lime green. And since late afternoon bulldozers had moved over from the rubble heaps and were attacking the stadium structure. The traffic of wrecking artels and heavy equipment was being directed by members of the Dog Society.

From their vantage point at the top of the berm, the two boys could see far below them benches and other paraphernalia of the Assembly being carried over and piled on top of the Congress. The fire pole at the center of the stage had already been lighted. It was crackling and the debris piled up around it was also beginning to flame.

In front of the forum of the Congress, senators of the Rotary Club were dancing. There were mummers—the Minutemen and Squatters—among them. All were performing the final Dance House.

And now the wooden stage of the Congress itself caught fire.

The boys suddenly felt awe.

A moment before they had been playing and running through the crowd. Now they stood still. The core of the stadium became a giant blaze under the night sky. A flare of light seemed to move upward from the center, illuminating the entire bowl. The bare and empty bleachers glowed like a bone.

A moment before there had been only the lighted pyres in the center of the field and the masked officers dancing around them at the base. Now the arena was empty. The heat had driven the dancing officials away to take refuge on the lower tiers.

The whole pyre flamed. A funnel of sparks shot directly up as if sucked by the sky and without cause, having nothing to do with the stadium at all. The officials stood isolated, as though shipwrecked. They looked out from the lowest tiers, as from a beach onto the sea. Behind them there was nothing. A void.

The senators and the mummers stood floodlighted.

Through the breaches in the earth dike the citizens of Garh had flowed in and filled the upper third of the great bowl, looking down at the scene, themselves lighted by the glowing sky.

Now came the final event of the Ten-Fourth, the razing of the speak houses. The globes of these structures were set to the torch one by one by the wreckers. Over the tiered seats they were like bright onion skins. The fabric had already been splashed with "wilderness" marks. These marks too flamed and crumpled.

Explosions rent the air. From the six sides gusts of material seemed to be heaved up over the spectators.

Srikant shut his eyes tight, then opened them in a daze.

"Spreccia! Spreccia!"

"Holy Fourth!"

"Energy!"

The people gave a shout.

•   •

The next day Blake, Morris, and Alvarez walked with the priest, Tutuola, as he went about his task of "sewing the ground." The destroyed Tenth was to be the seedbed for the new ward in Garh. The blue priesthood from throughout the Wilderness had come to conduct the ceremonies of renewal.

Evidently there was no single (and official) rite. In fact most of the residents of the city of Garh had left the burned-out quarter.

His bare feet muddy, Tutuola walked with a dignified mien through the encampment. There were long lines of tents where soup kitchens had been set up. He would stop every once in a while to speak to several of the new squatters.

To each group he would distribute his "wilderness branches." These would be planted immediately beside one of the shacks that had arisen miraculously during the night in large numbers. There seemed to have been some advance planning. Boundary lines of rudimentary streets between the rows of shacks were suggested.

In fact these new squatters who stood in shirt sleeves had been the property-owners and well-to-do burghers of the ward only a week before.

Blake and Morris carried bunches of branches.

In the lanes were puddles. The visitors noted that water from the canals had already been diverted by the engineers into the new settlement. The ground at Franklin Park had been trampled by the crowds the night before. It had been a scene of fire. The smoking mounds were now putting out their own dandelions and fireweed. The priest's weeds seemed not so much an addition to this local vegetation as its emblem.

Alvarez had fallen behind his companions; the two explorers returned to him now and again and then caught up with Tutuola. The filmmaker had had both ears cut off as a result of the judgment of the Noodlemakers. A large bandage covered these marks of the People's justice.

Still, Alvarez continued to wear his fatigue cap, slightly askew, and kept calling to his companions.

He was to be shipped off shortly to spend a year on the Sand Flats. However, as the term of exile had not yet begun, he had been allowed to attend this second episode of the Fire Festival.

The forest priest stopped to bless tools. Already a wall had been plastered, and the artel busy with this work had made certain technical drawings incised on the wet plaster, along with the "growth" mandalas.

Blake, familiar with the priest from the woods, noted in him a new potency.

The priest's gesture in blessing the production implements and planting the seed struck Blake as simple and natural. It was the Forest principle. An old stand of pine (which also had its periods of greater fecundity: "a good seed year") would reseed quickly an adjacent clearing. Probably the Deodars thought of themselves as ancient trees.

A group of squatters surrounded Tutuola. The group was

discussing the new form the ward might take. They thought the building material would be predominantly ferrochemical. However, it would take several years for production to get started on a large scale.

Residents wheeled up an electric generator. One of the bosses of the artel—a woman who was sending everyone scurrying—reminded Morris of Mrs. Zowie. Among the peers, an authority. He suspected the new institutions of the Ward would crystallize around such a person or group of persons. Of course the new institutions would be much the same. But what shape the new city would take he could not foresee.

In the mild afternoon the Wilderness men moved through the squatters' settlement and among the shanties. Now every roof sported its sacred weed, the Wilderness transplanted.

Beside one of the "soup" tents the American gypsies had set up a ferris wheel, and the wheeling gondolas were full of children. Underneath the machines were lines of other waiting children. They seemed to be mostly Karsts.

The Waste Land, flowering, had become a public park. Morris looked for Maddi in the line. But there were no Harditts. The Sawna people must have returned to rest in their Foreign Quarter.

Soon they too would be leaving Garh.

END OF BOOK II

Garh City is the second book of the tetralogy DAILY LIVES IN NGHSI-ALTAI.

The first two books were published, respectively, in 1977 and 1978 by New Directions. The final volumes will appear in the near future.

Red Shift: An Introduction to Nghsi-Altai (1977) has been published by Penny Each Press, Thetford, Vermont 05074.